M000240461

# Lifestyles Today

BRAUN

Chris van Uffelen

# Lifestyles Today

## Interior Design Around the World

# Contents

# Contents

# Introduction

In the last two years, people have spent an above-average amount of time at home. But it wasn't just the pandemic that made it abundantly clear how important our homes are. It has always been a place of retreat, relaxation, everyday life and family. In 2020, another function was added for many: the home often became the main workplace, and those who didn't want to work with virtual backgrounds now gave up part of their privacy. Still, even without conferencing on-line, the home had to take on office functions, and the sofa or dining table suddenly took on the function of a meeting room or desk. However, even apart from the expanded functions that the rooms had to take on completely unprepared, the much longer stay in the rooms made us aware of some inadequacies. So 2020 and 2021 probably became the years of interior design and numerous living spaces got an update. Those updates mostly concerned the apartment as a whole, its feel-good character and style. It was rarely aimed solely at creating a workspace, and if it was, then often just for interim use. These updates or new designs are intended not only to cope with the special situation of the pandemic but also to last far beyond it. More often, the living space was redesigned or remodeled as a living environment. This is the theme of this book: the variety of living options reflected in the interior - from compact and uncluttered to spacious and sophisticated, to ostentatious or playful. For every life plan there is a suitable living space and this must change with changes in personality or life circumstances as well. Of course, fashions and styles also play a role in the design process, and similar designs can suit very different situations. Thus, not everyone will find all of the designs in the book to be suitable for them, but everyone will find one or two designs that fit them exactly right now. The attentive reader will also discover designs – or parts of designs – that once matches him, and many can imagine a life that suits them for most of the projects. Accordingly, one of the goals of the book is also to discover oneself: Where can I live, where do I want to live, who would I be if I lived here?

# Penthouse L
## Vienna

Interior design and architecture
destilat Design Studio

Location
Vienna,
Austria

Year
2020

Gross floor area
200 m²

Number of bedrooms
3

An exciting interplay of luxurious materials and simple forms is the common thread running through the interior of the penthouse at the 9th and 10th floors of a new building. Many of the custom-made wooden fixtures have floating volumes. Plenty of storage space and hidden doors have been invisibly built into the walls using laminated walnut. The earthy wood elements form a clear contrast to the shiny bright floors and high-pile velour. The central element of the living room is the bioethanol fireplace. Slightly elevated, set in a light marble base, it is backed by a large-format, dark porcelain stoneware wall in marble look, which, in addition to the flames, also reflects the material aesthetics of classical modernism. Its base is the first step of the metal staircase to the upper floor, whose filigree strut railing makes the structure appear weightless.

a
Backlit round mirror in the hallway on wall of warm laminated walnut.

b
Hallway with staircase and fireplace.

c
Custom made furniture provide a place to relax near the bioethanol fireplace.

d
Lower floor plan.

e
Kitchen with clean bright surfaces, while the interior of the furniture is walnut.

f
The walk-in closet offers plenty of space.

g
Light fabrics divide the en-suite bathroom and walk-in closet from the bedroom.

# Shikor

Interior design and architecture
Spatial Architects

Location
Master Saber Ahmed Road,
Puichari, Banskhali, Chattogram,
Bangladesh

Year
2019

Gross floor area
446 m²

Number of bedrooms
4

Rooted in a Bangladeshi land, not far from commercial capital of the region, Chattogram, Shikor is a country house that rediscovers all the charm of rural lifestyle. The simplicity of forms use an architectural language that is at once perceivably timeless but bound to age and not decay as well. Bengali term Shikor, used to denote Roots: The origin from which it all begins. It is a celebration of what ties one to land. Shikor is a farmhouse on over 440 square meters that holds the legacy of the particular homestead, respects the features of traditional houses and celebrates the changes in nature. The build form creates an introvert environment considering highly conservative social context as well as creating a dialogue with an adjacent pond and the agricultural land.

Banskhali

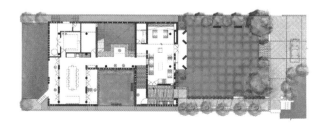

# The Starlake Villa

Interior design
Le House

Location
Hanoi,
Vietnam

Year
2018

Gross floor area
250 m²

Number of bedrooms
3

This house is fully focused on children playing. Play spaces where children can freely romp around can be discovered everywhere. The dark main color harmonizes with the light wooden elements. The interior design is characterized by a mixture of modern and classic elements. The architects have made it their goal to satisfy the needs of children with the interior design. Therefore, inconspicuous places were transformed into creative play spaces. This is also the case with the space under the stairs, which, thanks to its special design, invites children to play. Round openings in the walls replace ordinary doors and even make the way to the desk exciting. In this way, the barrier between learning and playing also disappears.

## Hanoi

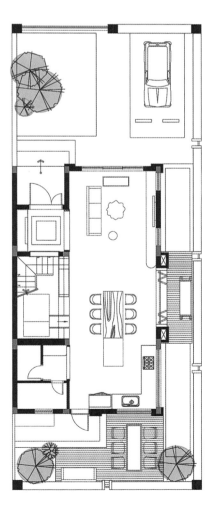

a

A creative solution was found for the space under the stairs, which gives the children plenty of room to play.

b

Round openings in the walls make the way to learning exciting.

c

The children's room is a colorful adventure land-scape where children can romp around.

d

The house is characterized by a dark color, which gives the rooms a modern appearance.

e

Ground floor plan.

# Reflections
# of the Past

**Interior design and architecture**
Firm architects

**Location**
Amsterdam,
The Netherlands

**Year**
2021

**Gross floor area**
94 m²

**Number of bedrooms**
2

The aim was to create an honest, masculine and architectural space with the largest possible usable floor area. To turn the unused old attic into a livable space, the previous owner raised the roof about fifty centimeters. This elevation on an old basis, has become the starting point for the creation. In the design, the entire space is visibly cut at a height of 95 centimeters above the floor. Above everything is new and covered in rendered and isolated walls; below it is bare and rough. The use of dark mirrors, unfinished zinc sheets and rough bricks creates a special composition of materials. The blurry zinc part above the line reflects a lot of light into the room. The dark mirrors reflect less light, but do give a sharp image.

Amsterdam

d

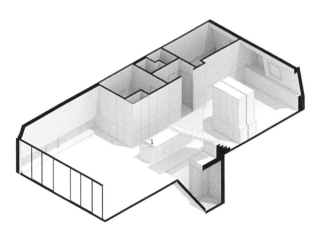

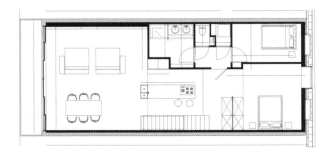

a
The horizontal line devides old and new.

b
Even the stairs change material at the old/new-line.

b
Dining table and view outside.

d
The line is located at the level of a central part of a man's body.

d
Literally the line shows people are rooted in the past and looking to the future.

e
Isometric drawing and floor plan.

# House F
## Frankfurt/Main

**Interior design**
Schmidt Holzinger Innenarchitekten

**Location**
Frankfurt/Main,
Germany

**Year**
2018

**Gross floor area**
470 m²

**Number of bedrooms**
2

Continuous, smooth ceiling surfaces create flowing room sequences on the ground floor and basement. The doors are frameless and room-high. Instead of conventional skirting boards, a shadow gap forms the transition from floor to wall. An ecru tone from the NCS color system forms the basis of the color and material design. This color tone is found in many building components and design elements. Room-high, dark furniture cubes made of smoked oak characterize the design of the living spaces. In the kitchen, the fronts and countertop of the cooking block are made of stainless steel. In the basement, the color ecru is combined with light sandstone and furniture made of walnut. In the dressing room, the sliding glass doors on the front sides are half-mirrored. The wardrobe doors on the long sides are covered with graphite horsehair.

e

f

a
Washbasin of the guest toilet.

b
Kitchen showing smoked oak cabinets.

c
Library with painting by Peter Seharsch.

d
Dressing room with half mirrored glass and horsehair doors.

e
TV wall in the living room.

f
Ground floor and basement plan.

# Villa
# Africa

Interior design and architecture
Arch Micol Maiga – Maiga Architetti

Location
Bordighera,
Italy

Year
2020

Gross floor area
2.050 m²

Number of bedrooms
6

Villa Africa is a tailor-made project. A study of the excavations and reinforced concrete, the technical components and the stratigraphy of the walls entailed the customization of two floors and creation of ad hoc furnishing elements. The living room window is protected by bronze and cedar wood sunshades. The interior furnishings are a mix of family pieces, flanked by comfortable upholstered furniture of primary Italian manufacture, combined with pieces specifically designed for the villa. Some of the elements evoke, in a modern key, the wooden furniture of the 1950s. Structural engineer of the project was Marco Bruzzone, and general building site management was done by Mya architect Andrea Russiello.

## Bordighera

d

e

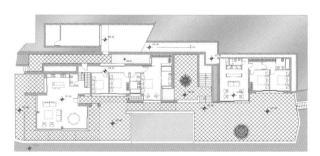

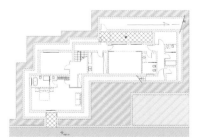

g

a
The outdoor seating area offers a generous view over the surrounding nature.

b
The outdoor pool area and its relaxing character.

c
The kitchen is made of backlit honey onyx, integrated with a teak wood storage part and emperador dark marble worktops.

d
The garden is a meeting of exotic and Mediterranean plants that enhance the space and make it unique and pleasant to live in.

e
The stair railing is a construction of thick glass that enhances the contrast of modern and vintage furniture in the villa.

f
Teak and oak furniture line the bathroom. The floors and wall tiles are made of natural stone all cut to size.

g
Ground and basement floor plan.

# Gem A
## Frankfurt/Main

Interior design and architecture
Simone Jüschke Innen|Architektur

Location
Frankfurt/Main

Year
2020

Gross floor area
496 m²

Number of bedrooms
5

An aging 1950s gem was given a modern look through careful renovation and a restrained design concept. The house in Frankfurt's West End was converted into a dream home for a young family. It was given a consistently modern look through careful refurbishment. High-quality materials and well thought-out interventions in the structure bring the house into the present while still maintaining its charm. The imposing entrance area received a new staircase and the luxurious air space received an eye-catcher with custom lighting and large-scale art. The individually planned built-in furniture supports the calm overall appearance and offers sufficient storage as well as space for the air conditioning system. The planning included guidance in the selection of loose furnishings and a selection of textiles. The design concept of the interior continues on the terrace and in the garden and is completed by a bicycle and storage shed in the outdoor area.

a
View across the hall from second floor to ground floor.

b
The staircase on the first floor with the artwork Vincent's Flowers (After van Gogh) by UK based artist Paul Wright, commissioned on the clients behalf placed by art consultancy firm Velvenoir.

c
View into the kitchen.

d
Ground and first floor plan.

e
Master bathroom on the second floor.

f
There is plenty of space for the dining room and the living room.

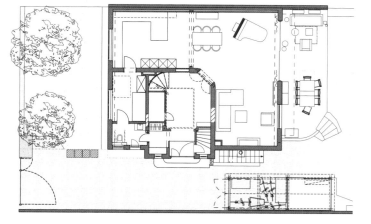

# Garden
# Villa

Interior design and architecture
Gabriela Raible Innenarchitektur
Planungsgesellschaft

Location
Grünwald, near Munich,
Germany

Year
2020

Gross floor area
450 m²

Number of bedrooms
4

From the single domicile of an elderly gentleman to a lively home for a family of four: A classic-modern villa built in 2002 in the south of Munich was completely transformed through modernization and redesign. Now, a strong connection from the annex to the main house, intelligently planned fixtures and plenty of storage space create structure and form the basis for communicative family life and hospitality. The calm, clear basic architectural concept with high-quality, natural materials and fine handcrafted details characterize the design. A special trait is the light, open view of the garden with the old tree population – a dream home come true for the architecture-affine owners. In regular, fruitful jour fixes, a villa with expressive effect and long-lasting aesthetics was created.

## Grünwald

a

High-quality wood panels increase the warmth of the fire place in the living area.

b

The light-flooded elegance of the living area invites to a good read.

c

Doors of delicately framed glass panes offer a view from the corridor into the garden.

d

Floor plan.

e

The fire place in the center of the room separates the living from the dining area and yet allows unhindered communication.

f

The swimming pool in the wellness is reminiscent of a Roman spa.

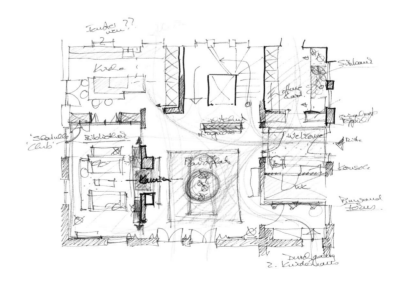

d

# The Wonderland Park Residence

Interior design
Alexander Design

Architecture
Assembledge+

Location
Laurel Canyon, CA
USA

Year
2018

Gross floor area
302 m²

Number of bedrooms
4

Nestled in the hills of the Laurel Canyon, The Wonderland Park Residence is situated within an enclave of mid-century residences from which it draws its inspiration. Originally a ranch house built in 1956, the project entails an upper-floor addition and extensive remodel. A narrow, nine-meter long skylight mediates between the original pitched roof and the volume of the new addition where it rises to the first floor. This brings light and geometric clarity to the spaces, further enhanced by the Western Red Cedar cladding that runs continuously from the ceiling of the family room up through the skylight and around the exterior walls of the second story. The kitchen is the heart of the residence, physically connecting the social and private areas and providing views horizontally to the landscape and vertically through the skylight.

Laurel Canyon

b

a
While the eastern part of the living room is completely glazed, a closed wall with a fireplace screens the area to the south.

b
The family room opens up to the swimming pool.

c
The courtyard is framed by walls to keep privacy and create a calm atmosphere.

d
Ground and first floor plan.

e
The furniture blends in with the architecture.

f
The open space on ground floor allows views from the kitchen across the dining room to the living room.

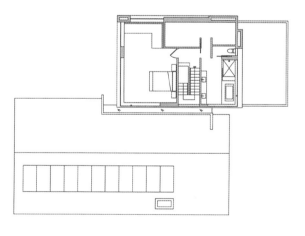

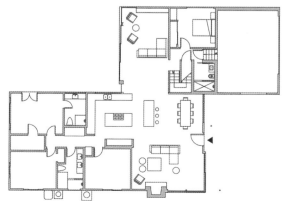

d

# Mountain Charme

**Interior design**
Go Interiors

**Location**
Plazza da Scoula, 7500 St. Moritz,
Switzerland

**Year**
2021

**Gross floor area**
182 m²

**Number of bedrooms**
3

Both floors of the Penthouse Plazza were originally planned as office space and were taken over in the shell – without walls and stairs. With great sensitivity, the architects created a beautiful, luxurious retreat in the middle of one of the most beautiful areas of the Swiss Alps. According to their company philosophy of creating emotions, they succeeded in creating a home away from home. The condensation of the surface, the use of precious and tactile-sensual materials in combination with skillful lightening create coziness and warmth. Sensuality and the claim of feeling at home are the core goals of their work. With this extraordinary project, they created an inspiring and enriching living experience for their clients out of nothing.

## St. Moritz

a
Warmth becomes palpable in the shades of brown, gray and black that dominate the living room.

b
Visitors may enjoy alpine charm in the guest bedroom.

c
The stairs lead from the fourth up to the fifth floor.

d
In the master bedroom, a special mix of textile materials provides ultimate coziness.

e
Fourth floor plan.

f
A private spa forms a treasure within the house.

a

# Kvitfjell
# Cabin

Interior design and architecture
Erling Berg

Location
Svartskardvegen 178, Fåvang,
Norway

Year
2021

Gross floor area
145 m²

Number of bedrooms
4

Nestled in the landscape on the top of Kvitfjell in Norway, this narrow cabin stretches 26 meters to frame the views of the surrounding. Using traditional methods of construction, the entire cabin is built out of local pine wood. The exterior is wrapped in untreated wood panels that will naturally gray over time. The entire interior is wrapped in white oiled pine, keeping the spaces light. Although every main room in the cabin has a southwest view, bedrooms and bathrooms are kept discreet, with storage in the walls, leaving more space for the open kitchen, dining and family room. Following the topography of the plot, the main living spaces and the en-suite are lowered in the landscape, with vaulted ceilings, creating a spacious atmosphere where the cold nature outside connects with the warm interior through the larger glass openings.

Fåvang

c

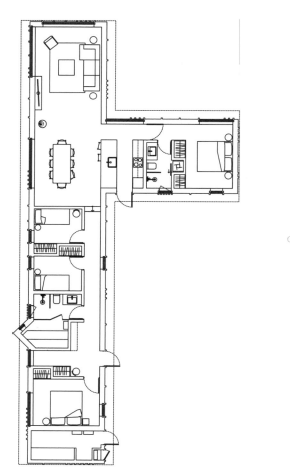

d

a
View into the bright and spacious dining and family room.

b
The interior design keeps the cabin cozy, even when it's covered in snow.

c
Western side of the narrow cabin.

d
Ground floor plan.

e
White pine wood keeps the room bright even in the dark winter hours.

# Highland
# House

**Interior design and architecture**
Coates Design: Architecture + Interiors

**Location**
Issaquah, WA,
USA

**Year**
2020

**Gross floor area**
458,5 m²

**Number of bedrooms**
3

Architectural simplicity inspired this special home in the beautiful Issaquah Highlands. A large central core with double-high ceilings anchors the heart of the home with two wings on either side. A gable roof creates a contemporary take on a classic design. Concrete floors extend throughout the first story and white walls are accented with light hardwood cabinetry. Bumblebee yellow drawers in the kitchen provide a splash of color to the interior. The kitchen and a large living area anchor the heart of the home. The east wing is designated for family activities. The west wing is home to the garage. This home exemplifies a classic design implemented through the balanced integration of modern features.

## Issaquah

a
Warm touches of bumblebee yellow in the kitchen mirror the warmth of the fire burning in the chimney.

b
Vast windows and generous sliding glass doors fill the interior with natural light. The modern gable roof allows for a seamless transition from wall to ceiling.

c
The east wing includes a 56 square-meter exercise/sunroom, a large swimming pool and a ping-pong table.

d
An U-shaped floating staircase transports occupants to the second floor where a hardwood skybridge divides the master bedroom from the other two bedrooms.

e
Ground floor plan.

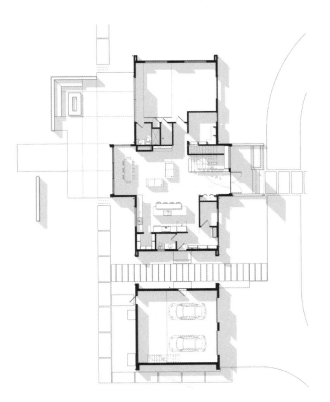

# A Home for Readers

Interior design
ATOMAA

Location
Milan,
Italy

Year
2019

Gross floor area
95 m²

Number of bedrooms
1

High above the treetops of one of the most beautiful streets in Milan, the sun fills an apartment with light, where functionality and aesthetics compete for the throne. The house, designed and built in fall 2019, narrates the story of those who live within: a young couple with a passion for reading, cinema, design and music. The act of opening continues throughout the home through a series of large portal doors. The latter, however, completely integrated into a long bookcase, hides panels of an intense yellow, which provide a defined division between the entertainment and private spaces. The project, while not upsetting the original layout of the house, gives the new owners flexible spaces, brightness, wide fields of view and a succession of varied environments that are always in communication with each other.

Milan

e

f

g

a
A colorful and cozy living space.

b
A furnished wall doubles as a portal to the more private parts of the home.

c
A furnished wall acts as a threshold between living room and study.

c
A sun-filled reading niche.

e
View to the bedroom.

f
A game of contrasting colors brings life to the bathroom while overlapping curves maintain a playful theme.

g
Floor plan.

a

# Villa Schatzlmayr

Interior design and architecture
Philipp Architekten

Location
Passau,
Germany

Year
2019

Gross floor area
760 m²

Number of bedrooms
2

A spacious, ground-level domicile with a view of nature - Villa Schatzlmayr is a three-part ensemble. With a floor-to-ceiling glass front, the building opens up to the landscape. The center is the lounge-like living area with open kitchen, dining and fireplace room. A glass joint branches off from this into the sleeping quarters with master bedroom, master bath, dressing room and fitness room. A two-story cube marks the studio building. The infinity pool stretches into the building and visually merges with the horizon in the garden. The interior is reduced and timelessly designed: Natural hues and high-quality materials such as the sand-colored stone floor, walnut wood furnishings and cognac-colored Chesterfield leather sofas give the rooms character. This is matched by the kitchen in white with gray details. Bright colors surprise in the basement.

Passau

d

e

a
The uninterrupted floor-to-ceiling glazing opens up views of the surrounding landscape.

b
The chesterfield sofa and walnut furniture create a characterful and warm room.

c
A chandelier above the dining table adds a slightly playful accent.

d
Contrasting with the restrained design of the building, the guest toilet with skylight is designed in pink.

e
The master bathroom with a freestanding bath-tub.

f
Ground floor plan.

f

# High-Park Residence

a

Interior design and arrchitecture
Batay-Csorba Architects

Location
Toronto, Ontario,
Canada

Year
2020

Gross floor area
325 m²

Number of bedrooms
4

Built for an Italian couple, the design pays homage both to the clients' Italian heritage and that of the Toronto residential building fabric, while ensuring a sensitivity towards wellbeing, mobility, and convenience. The vault is one of the most common archetypes of ancient Roman architecture, characterized by its powerful modulation of light and its sense of lightness. In adopting this typology into a domestic space, Batay-Csorba Architects evolved the vault from its primary form, puncturing, cutting and peeling it into new geometries that help to distribute light and air into key locations, respond to program organization, demarcating each with a different atmosphere, and create a sectional continuity throughout the house.

Toronto

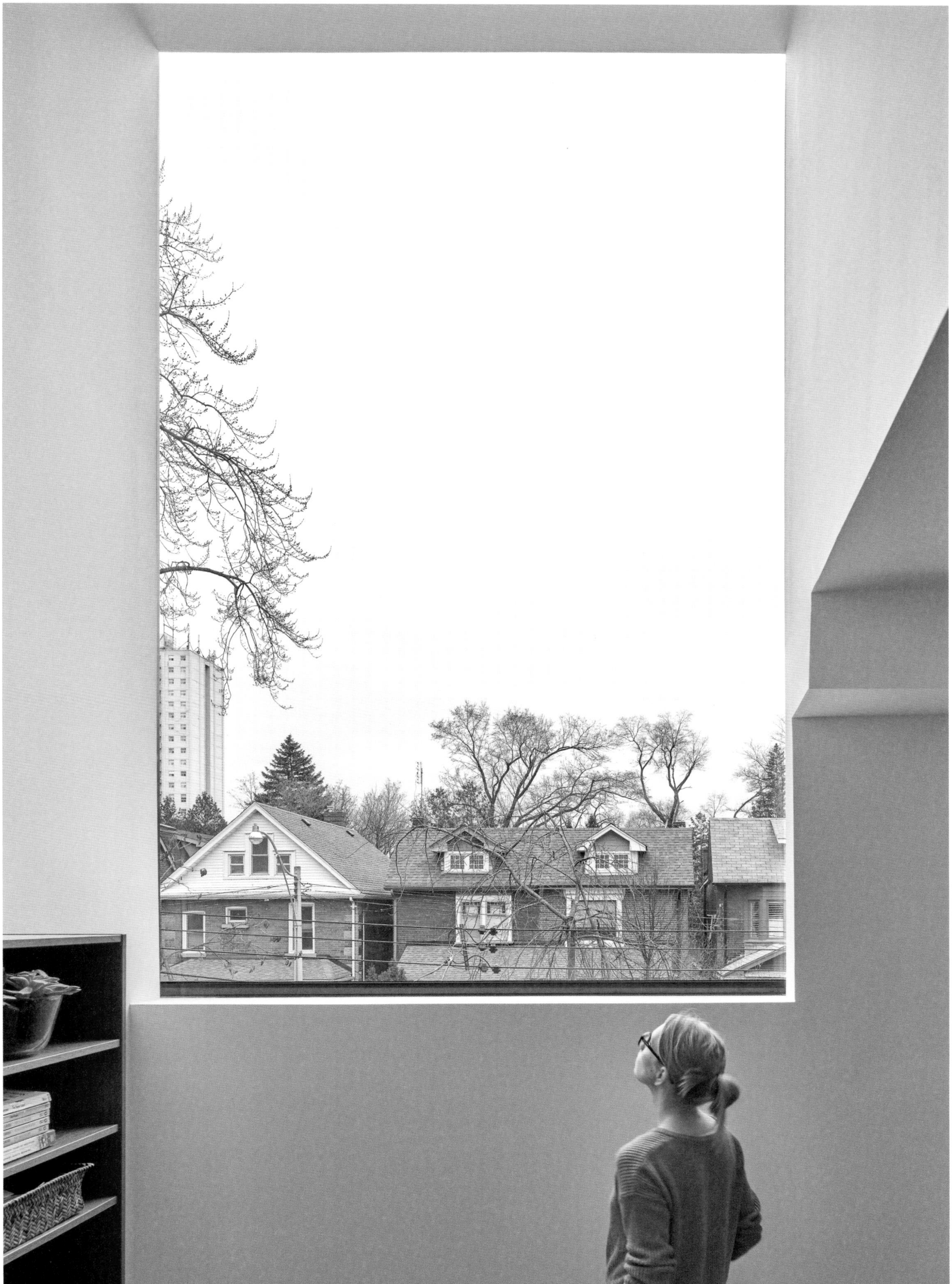

b

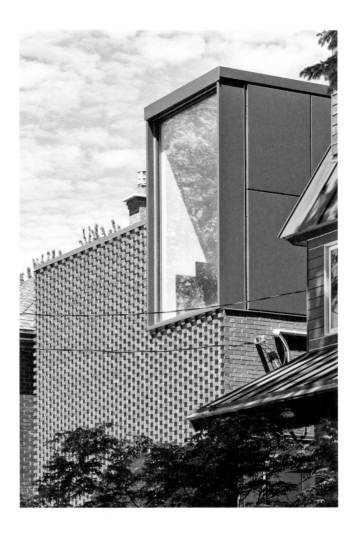

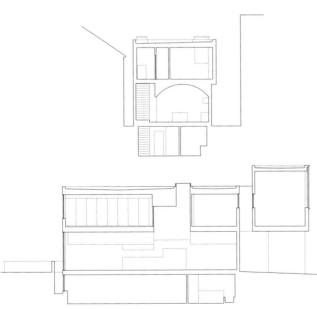

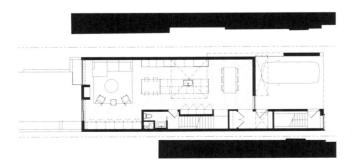

a
Living room with fireplace.

b
The large bay window provides light but shelters as well.

c
The vault spanning over the kitchen.

d
Daylight falling into the basement .

e
The large window towers .

f
The large window rises above the closed brick-work.

g
Sections and ground floor plan.

# Holiday
# House

Interior design and architecture
blocher partners

Location
Lake Constance,
Germany

Year
2020

Gross floor area
570 m²

Number of bedrooms
5

Nestled against the slope as if it wants to hide, only to over-whelm with full force on entering: The vacation home with boathouse character on the shores of Lake Constance impressively merges interior and exterior. Both the purist-looking gable roof and a large part of the façade are clad in shingled cedar wood. Glazing to the south and west opens up the facade, while only a few views are offered to the street side. As closed as the building presents itself to the street, it is open inside through floor-to-ceiling panoramic windows that offer a view of the lake. The interior design is therefore deliberately restrained and concentrates on the essentials: Natural materials enter into an aesthetic symbiosis with a re-duced color palette that knows how to set individual accents.

## Lake Constance

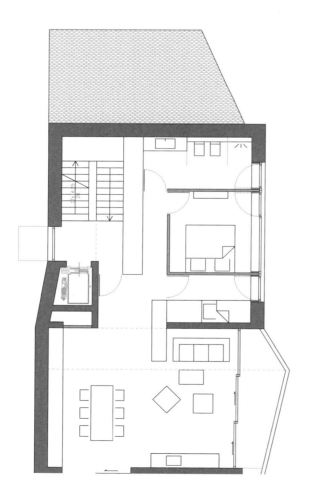

a
The shingled façade embeds the house into the surrounding nature.

b
Floor-to-ceiling panorama windows in the living quarters give the feeling that the inside and the outside meld.

c
The ceilings and walls are made of fair-faced concrete that has partly been rendered in white to correspond with the limestone floors.

d
The interior design focuses on the essentials – an aesthetic symbiosis arises of natural materials and a muted color scheme bar a few highlights.

e
Ground floor plan.

f
The living area is extended onto the lake by a pier-like balcony.

# 0711-Maisonette
## Stuttgart

**Interior design and architecture**
Cyrus Ghanai

**Location**
Stuttgart,
Germany

**Year**
2020

**Gross floor area**
198 m²

**Number of bedrooms**
2

High above the rooftops of Stuttgart lies this maisonette with a spectacular view. It includes a kitchen, living room, dining room, bedroom, dressing room, guest rooms, bathrooms, adjoining rooms and a spacious outdoor area. To emphasize the open character of the apartment, the designer completely redesigned and moved the kitchen area on the lower floor. All the fixtures as well as the wardrobe in the dressing room were designed with a perfect fit and with an exquisite finish. A highlight is the new lit staircase, which blends harmoniously into the rest of the apartment. In developing the color concept, the designer incorporated the natural color palette of the surroundings. Iridescent gray, at times metallic, at times pale blue, and yellow hues from strong olive to brass colors are complemented by a few contrasting colors. In selecting the loose furniture, the designer focused on high-quality pieces and tactile fabrics.

a
Natural colors and haptic textiles add to the coziness of the living room.

b
The dining area and terrace offer a wide view across the rooftops of the city.

c
The maisonette hosts a spacious kitchen with elegant black and white furnishings.

d
Upper and lower floor plan.

e
The stairs leading to the upper floor are warmly lit.

f
Purposefully placed skylights bring a sunny day or a starry night into the bedroom.

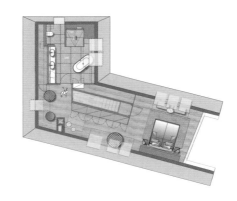

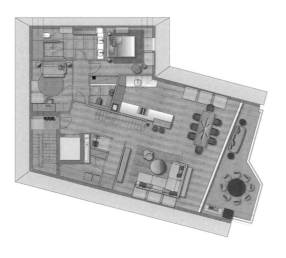

# House in Nakagyo Area

**Interior design**
koyori

**Location**
Kyoto,
Japan

**Year**
2020

**Gross floor area**
90 m²

**Number of bedrooms**
3

Due to the corona pandemic, people spend much more time in their homes. For this reason, the architect has created a cozy home for his family. The house in Nakagyo is a 40-year-old apartment building made of reinforced concrete in the heart of Kyoto. The house provides a homey place where the family can play together, do homework and spend some quiet hours together. The windows are made of frosted glass to adequately separate the private area from the public while allowing enough light into the house. Traditional construction methods and natural materials, Japanese paper with a touch of handwork and plaster finish characterize the aesthetics of the house. The materials age over time and change with the growth of the family's children.

a
The combination of natural materials and traditional construction creates a cozy home.

b
The center of the house is the kitchen island, which takes up most of the space.

c
In the kitchen the parents can cook without losing sight of the children.

d
Thanks to the frosted glass windows, the rooms are flooded with light and at the same time guarantee the privacy of the family.

e
Floor plan.

f
View of the modern minimalist bathroom.

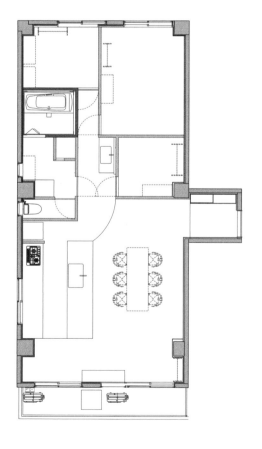

# T3

Interior design
Cubo design architect

Architecture
Hitoshi Saruta Architect

Location
Kamakura City,
Japan

Year
2019

Gross floor area
507 m²

Number of bedrooms
3

This house was designed for an international couple, a French artist and his Japanese wife. It's a place for them to settle and live permanently as well as to invite guests from overseas. The house is nestled quietly atop a hill in the historic Japanese city Kamakura, which is facing wonderful scenery of the Shonan coastline with distant views of an iconic peak of Mount Fuji. The façade is completely closed to the street by a concrete wall to create privacy, while it is fully opened in the direction of the landscape, so that the focus lies on the majestic nature and wonderful scenery only. The characteristically continuous eaves, which function to protect from the rain and direct sunlight were added in a modern way. While using traditional Japanese materials, such as granite, Japanese paper, black plaster, wood lattice and louvers Japanese features can be felt.

Kamakura City

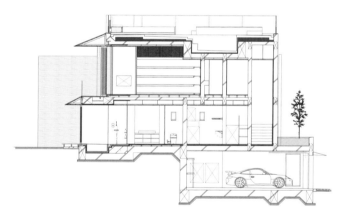

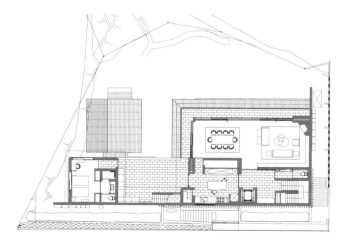

a
The wide living room area with its punctual arranged gloomy lights which create a feeling of warmth in the evening hours.

b
The traditional eaves were designed in a modern way by making it sharp and thin while adopting steel plate in structure and finish.

c
The master bedroom is flooded with light from the courtyard.

d
Cross section and first floor plan.

e
Panoramic windows in the living room offer a generous view over the majestic surrounding nature.

f
The bathroom for guests picks up on the traditional Japanese aesthetic which can be experienced individually by visitors.

# Monastery House

a

Interior design
Bureau Fraai

Architecture
Nicolaas Nelis

Location
Bennebroek,
The Netherlands

Year
2018

Gross floor area
340 m²

Number of bedrooms
4

In the former Saint Lucia monastery from 1896 in Bennebroek, the Netherlands, Bureau Fraai has created a design that transforms a characteristic monastery into a high quality family home, while retaining the characteristic features of the monastery. A new oak staircase with a slim steel railing connects the living room to the basement on one side, and the bedrooms for the children and the multifunctional attic on the other. The introduction of a robust oak element in this attic divides the large space with authentic beams into a sleeping area with Jacuzzi, a bathroom, a walk-in closet and a mezzanine with workstations. The bed and whirlpool are nestled in a raised platform.

## Bennebroek

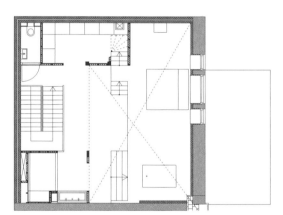

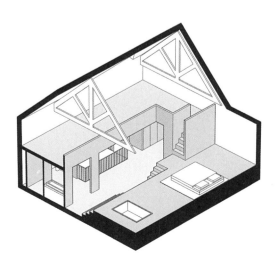

a
The sturdy oak element divides the large room into sections.

b
Modern elements transform the special monastery building into a cozy family home.

c
In the modern bathroom, the element of oak is picked up again, creating a visual connection with the other rooms.

d
The staircase with a slender steel railing creates the connection between the floors.

e
Floor plan and isometric drawing.

# Prefabricated
## Stuttgart

Interior design and architecture
Lee+Mir Architekten

Location
Stuttgart,
Germany

Year
2021

Gross floor area
450 m²

Number of bedrooms
1

Built in 1921, the architects gave the house a completely new look by remodeling and extending it. They restructured the room functions, added a pool and created a modern and noble home. Inside, custom walnut cabinets simultaneously divide and connect the dressing room, kitchen and living room. A fireplace separates the dining room from the living area, but at the same time allows generous through views. The kitchen's precast concrete countertop flows into the fireplace's seating area, creating a connection between the spaces. Prefabricated, anthracite-colored precast concrete elements define the overall look of the home. Acoustic panels in the ceilings reduce sound and joints serve as a source of light. Filigree window profiles merge the interior and exterior. The wellness area is connected to the garden by a staircase with an integrated whirlpool. The building is heated and cooled with earth energy. The electricity is produced by a photo-voltaic system.

a
Joints structure the wall cladding.

b
The modern fireplace.

c
The outside pool is the focal point of the interiors.

d
Design classics go along with contemporary pieces.

e
Ground floor plan.

f
Natural materials around the pool.

g
Even the bathroom offers a view to the pool.

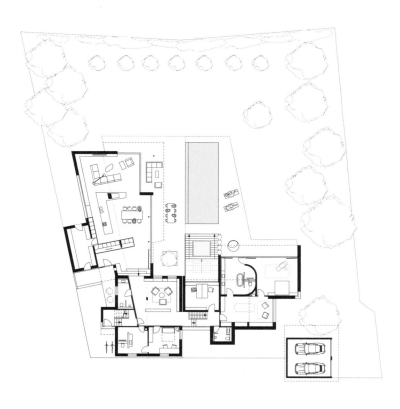

e

# Penthouse
# Steger

Interior design
atelier INTI and Leonie Olivia Schima

Architecture
Daniel Böpple Architekt

Location
Friedrichshain, Berlin,
Germany

Year
2020

Gross floor area
250 m²

Number of bedrooms
3

This bright penthouse apartment in Berlin-Friedrichshain was realized according to the wishes of the owner family. The modern color and material concept and all installations were individually designed. The light-flooded and warm appearance of the apartment is mainly based on the continuous, white oiled oak herringbone parquet flooring and the matching fixtures and the large dormer windows, as well as the skylights. The apartment is divided into a spacious living/dining area with kitchen unit and a private area, a separately accessible apartment, the wellness oasis, and the guest bathroom are in the back. From the living/dining area, a light-filled stair-case provides access to the roof terrace. In the bathrooms, large-format tiles emphasize the spaciousness of the rooms.

# Berlin

a
View into the master bathroom revealing the free-standing bath tub and wooden closets.

b
A built-in cabinet for washing machine and dryer, as well as the vanity cabinet and the privacy slats were made of fine walnut wood.

c
The countertops in a light marble look and the cabinet fronts in dark bog oak, create an elegant contrast.

d
Sections of the guest bathroom.

e
The particularly extravagant guest bathroom is filled with a tropical atmosphere.

f
In the entrance area of the apartment, a large built-in wardrobe offers plenty of storage space and a seating niche.

g
View from the open kitchen into the corridor.

e

f

g

# Single Family House with Poolhouse

Interior design
Studio Ambacht with Oostkaai

Architecture
David D'Hulst

Location
Lier,
Belgium

Year
2015

Gross floor area
320 m²

Number of bedrooms
3

Located on the border between urban development and rural area, the thoroughly renovated farm pays tribute to the designers Le Corbusier, Louis Kahn and Carlo Scarpa. On entering, the visitor will catch a glimpse of a swimming pool and a black pool house at the back of the garden. A central atrium connected to the hallway supplies the house with sunlight. The six-meter-high courtyard walls are in stark contrast to the 2.26-meter-high kitchen: the golden ratio of Le Corbusier. The kitchen forms a lookout over the entire house and garden. An eye-catching bookshelf connects it with the living area on a lower level. Walnut, dark oak and brown marble were used alongside polished concrete for the floors and exposed concrete for the ceilings. The façades of white painted brick, concrete and exotic afrormosia wood are inspired by Kahn.

Lier

d

e

a

From the outside, the play of different levels and color contrasts is clearly visible.

b

The bed is placed in the room as a cozy niche and reflects the eye-catching bookshelves.

c

The central atrium with pending lights of Alvar Aalto.

d

A shower of sunlight falls into the bathroom and contrasts with the dark brown painted walls.

e

A long swimming pool leads to a small wooden house in the garden which serves as holiday home or home office.

f

First floor plan.

f

# Gentle Remodeling

**Interior design**
Eham

**Location**
Tegernsee,
Germany

**Year**
2020

With the desire to create a coherent living and dining area, 97 square meters of the house were remodeled. Previously, the kitchen and living room were isolated from each other. Now an overlapping space unites the living and dining areas. The Jerusalem Stone floor in the kitchen was retained, creating a connection to the original furnishings. The Ceppo marble kitchen island combined with the oak fronts give the kitchen a contemporary design. Black steel supports the shelving above the kitchen island as well as the solid oak table top. The former tiled stove is now just bricked up and has a restrained appearance. The floor in the dining and living areas is made of soaped oak and the furnishings of the living area with a sofa set and a wall of shelves are also simple and elegant.

## Tegernsee

a
Gently remodeling the kitchen combines traditional materials with contemporary design.

b
Large windows and glass doors bring the picturesque wild garden into the kitchen.

c
The modernized tiled stove connects the living and dining areas.

d
Sketch of the kitchen and ground floor plan with color marked area that was remodeled.

e
The outdoor annex prepares space for a cozy family gathering around the fireplace.

f
The spacious living area offers space for a relaxing evening.

# Court House in Erl

a

Interior design and architecture
Architekt Torsten Herrmann

Location
Jauch 14, 6343 Erl,
Austria

Year
2020

Gross floor area
1,595 m²

Number of bedrooms
3

In a dense residential area, the aim was to create privacy and the possibility of protected outdoor space despite the proximity. The building is divided into two wings. In between, there is a narrower connecting part that combines the two volumes. This U-shaped plan creates an organization of rooms around a private courtyard. It opens to the south and becomes the central outdoor space. An exposed concrete frame partially covers the terrace and traces the separation of the floors, as well as the contour of the courtyard. On the first floor, adjacent to the entrance, there is a spacious cooking and dining area, and in the rear wing, slightly lowered and pushed into the slope, there is the living room. On the upper floor the parents' suite is orientated towards the street, in the slope-side part of the building are the children's rooms.

Erl

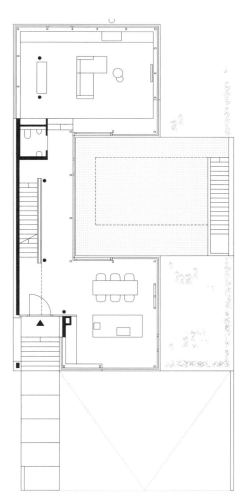

a
Living room with fireplace.

b
View to the dining place and the courtyard.

c
View from living room across the courtyard to the dining room.

d
The corridor with the staircases runs along behind the courtyard.

e
Ground floor plan.

# House with
# the Birds

Interior design
Marina Kutepova

Location
454000, White Rosy Village,
Chelyabinsk Region,
Russia

Year
2018

Gross floor area
135 m²

Number of bedrooms
2

The hostess of this country house wanted to add the simplicity of the village style and closeness to nature to the interior. The main style has become English country, but in the bedroom and guest room one can also see the style of chalet and Provence. Lamps and tableware made of aged copper and bronze, figurines and paintings were chosen as accessories. Pillows, carpets, and ornaments on the walls bring coziness to the atmosphere. Around the blue sofa and the fireplace a recreation area was built, to which the kitchen space adjoins and becomes part of a single whole. Large windows overlook the courtyard, which allowed the Interior Designer to decorate the room with shutters. The fireplace and the TV are placed in a way that they can be watched even from the kitchen.

## Chelyabinsk

f

g

h

a
Cozy blankets, pillows and bright colors create a pleasant atmosphere.

b
An impressive glass cabinet is placed in the hallway.

c
Painted ornaments by Victoria Pitirimova on the wooden walls decorate the bedroom.

d
View into the cozy kitchen.

e
The recreation area is formed around the blue sofa.

f
The style of the country house is preserved and made homely by a warm interior design.

g
Numerous pictures are placed over the sanitary facilities in the rustic bathroom.

h
Ground floor plan.

# La Extraviada
## Mazunte

**Interior design**
Gala Sánchez-Renero

**Architecture**
em-estudio

**Location**
Mermejita Beach, Mazunte, Oaxaca,
Mexico

**Year**
2020

**Gross floor area**
472 m²

**Number of bedrooms**
4

Overlooking the Pacific Ocean, La Extraviada is built on the side of the hill in front of Mermejita beach. The house was designed taking into account the sea view and the air flow that keeps the rooms fresh. The volumetry of the project results from the superposition of volumes with large windows, one above the other, forming terraces and shaded overhangs. The social area is enclosed in a pavilion with a wooden structure and a roof covered with clay tiles, which opens onto the terrace that faces the sea. Two of the four rooms are integrated into the main building and two act as independent studios, as they have their own access and each has a kitchen and a private swimming pool. Regional woods and stones from nearby quarries have been used. The walls have a polished cement finish with brown pigments. The choice of materials allows the architecture to blend in with the colors of the surrounding nature near the majestic beach of Mermejita.

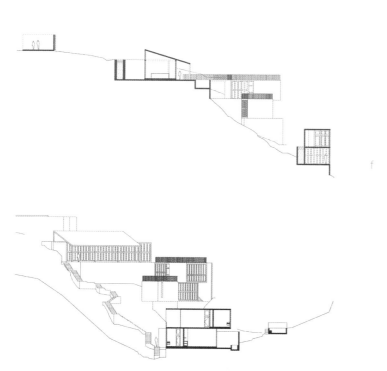

a
The volumes perfectly integrate into the surrounding landscape.

b
The building consists of volumes that lie on top of each other.

c
The social area is framed by large wooden doors with shutters.

d
Cross section plans.

d
The social area offers enough space to come together.

e
The bathroom and its neutral and calming colors.

f
The private studios are furnished individually and include a kitchen.

# Waldlerhaus 20.20.

a

**Interior design and architecture**
fabi architekten

**Location**
Viechtach,
Germany

**Year**
2020

**Gross floor area**
231 m²

**Number of bedrooms**
3

The traditional Bavarian Waldlerhaus consisted of a connected cooking/dining/living area with a tiled stove and an adjoining sleeping chamber. An entrance hall with ladder access to the wooden attic (Dachstadl) separated the house from the stable below. Taking up these traditions, the new building houses a large cooking/dining/living area with a central fireplace. On the wood-paneled upper floor, the individual rooms are located. Below, there are two additional study rooms with exterior access to the north slope. Horizontal windows to the northern forest side frame the panorama and bring the view including a castle ruin into the house. The materials mix modern, clear elements like exposed concrete and raw steel with traditional and original textures like oak wood floors.

Viechtach

d

e

a
A central fireplace replaces the traditional tiled stove.

b
The dining area is connected to the kitchen.

c
The staircase leading to the upper floor is reminiscent of the traditional ladder access.

d
Horizontal windows offer a view across the Bavarian Forest.

e
The bathroom is located on the upper floor.

f
Lower floor plan.

a

# Villa F

## Medebach

Interior design and architecture
ChristophHesseArchitekten

Location
Medebach,
Germany

Year
2017

Gross floor area
190 m²

Number of bedrooms
1

Ensuring energy efficiency and environmental protection are the key elements of the design of Villa F. The supply and disposal of the building are self-sufficient, therefore "off-the-grid", due to the owner's biogas plant nearby. The project functions as a system changer. Due to the exemplary character of the residential building, the entire village has in the meantime been connected to the local heating network of the farm. The house has two floors. The first floor houses office spaces of the biogas plant, while the loft-like upper floor houses the private living quarters. The building owners have demonstrated their creativity in their self-designed façade with stones from the nearby creek, which they use to continuously develop the building.

a
The stones from a nearby creek worked into the façade contrast with the smooth plaster of the exterior.

b
On entering the house visitors catch a glimpse of the biogas plant behind.

c
A water basin of stones placed in a lookout towards a creek valley connects the house with the source of its material.

d
Ground and first floor plan.

e
Smooth granite walls line the bathroom which is filled from above with natural light.

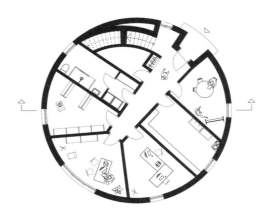

# Brand New
# Family Home

Interior design and architecture
Schneider | Architekten

Location
Sankt Georgen im Schwarzwald,
Germany

Year
2019

Gross floor area
500 m²

Number of bedrooms
4

The plot of the house borders directly on the forest in the east. The house offers the residents various, protected outdoor spaces. The double garage in front serves as a roof terrace. The access walkway to the house leads centrally to the staircase on the lower floor. On the uphill side are technical and cellar rooms and an access to the garage. The living and dining room and the kitchen are located on the upper floor. In the attic, the parents' area and two children's rooms are arranged along the west side. Galleries in all three rooms offer retreat areas. The building parts, that are in contact with the soil are made of reinforced concrete. The rest of the building is a timber frame construction with an untreated silver fir strip formwork. The floor consists of oiled oak plank flooring.

# Sankt Georgen

a
From the roof terrace, residents can enjoy the view of the city of Sankt Georgen im Schwarzwald.

b
The roof terrace in front of the building visually enlarges these lounges and allows the interior and exterior spaces to merge.

c
The double garage and roof terrace as well as the central rooms are oriented to the west.

d
The white, smoothly plastered walls in the interior harmonize with the oak flooring.

e
Cross section and lower floor plan.

f
House and garage enclose a courtyard carrying the roof terrace.

g
The kitchen can be separated from the open living and dining room.

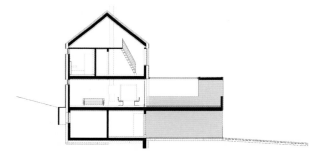

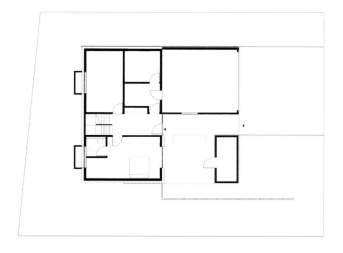

# Casa
# UC

Interior design and architecture
Daniela Bucio Sistos // Taller de
arquitectura y diseño

Location
Morelia, Michoacán,
Mexico

Year
2021

Gross floor area
550 m²

Number of bedrooms
4

Casa UC is a residence designed by Daniela Bucio Sistos, the architectural design arises from the concern to create a project with certain spatial ambiguity between the interior and exterior. It was sought to create a residence almost monochromatic but full of textures that with the incidence of natural light on the different volumes, the project would have different personalities throughout the day. Slender volumes distributed on a plan to create voids and courtyards that rise above masonry walls in the form of a slope. Upon entering and descending the access ramp, one finds the main foyer of the residence which is dressed with a tabachin in the center and a large circular elevated roof. The circular foyer is the guiding axis of the residence, and symbolically it is taken as the starting point for the radial floor that runs throughout the project.

Morelia

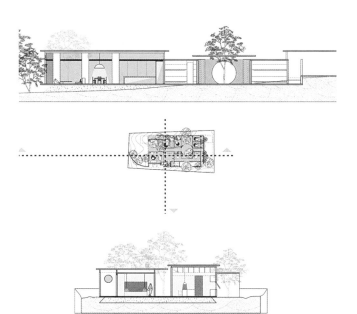

a
The openly designed façade offers a constant symbiosis of interior and exterior.

b
The tabachin in the center of the axis promotes a connection to nature, even on the inside.

c
The dining area is enriched by multiple textures and materials.

d
The spacious living room catches different variations of light during the day.

e
Ground floor plan and cross sections.

# Triangle
# Rectangle House

**Interior design and architecture**
Architect-k

**Location**
Yangsan, Gyeongsangnam-do,
South Korea

**Year**
2019

**Gross floor area**
208 m²

**Number of bedrooms**
3

The client of the triangular-rectangular house wanted a personal sanctuary to relax from city life. The hardship of the private area and the surroundings reflect the social attitude of the house. To create a balance between personal life and the environment, the architects created an enclosed courtyard. The interior of the house is designed to create a multitude of windows. The openings allow light to pass through. Direct and indirect light are separated and controlled to create subtle changes depending on the time of day. The light in the triangular house allows the occupants to face nature and come to rest in a time of tranquility. The exposed concrete, which serves as the interior finish becomes a smooth canvas for the light in the house.

Yangsan

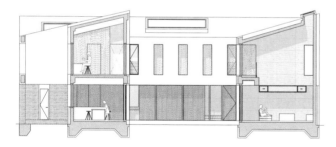

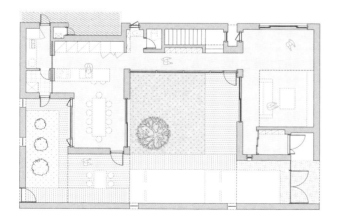

a
The house offers a retreat and exudes the tranquility that residents long for.

b
Natural light flows through the house through many openings and the skylight.

c
The courtyard brings the environment into the personal space and at the same time preserves its confidentiality.

d
The combination of concrete and wood creates a noble bathroom.

e
Section and first floor plan.

# House
# FX

Interior design, architecture and
landscape architecture
Fuchs, Wacker. Architekten

Location
Stuttgart,
Germany

Year
2017

Gross floor area
600 m²

Number of bedrooms
5

Two listed bungalows were merged into a spacious family residence with great respect and attention to detail. Past and present, art and architecture, inside and outside merge the two bungalows from 1969 by Kammerer and Belz while keeping the floor plans unchanged. The exposed brickwork has been freshly painted, the roof insulated, but the pool, wood ceilings and natural stone floors inside were allowed to remain. Existing niches were supplemented with custom built-ins. The rooms flow smoothly into one another – the walls are only room dividers – and end with a view of the Rems Valley. The light and nature from outside are brought into the living spaces via the 3.80-meter-high window walls and two large courtyards. With its clean lines and minimalist aesthetics, the post-war bungalow continues to inspire modern buildings.

Stuttgart

a
Living room with view to valley of the Rems.

b
Entrance at the slope.

c
Living and dining area.

d
Bedroom, courtyard and bathroom.

e
Sketch ground floor plan.

f
Master bathroom.

g
Extended living space.

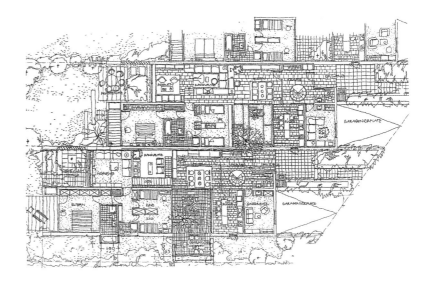

d

e

# Pinion House

a

Interior design and architecture
Ivo Mareines and Rafael Patalano

Location
Campos do Jordão,
Brazil

Year
2016

Gross floor area
1,300 m²

Number of bedrooms
5

The architect's first intention with the design of Pinion House was to avoid the widespread local European-alp style. The shape of the upper roof is sprouted like a fallen pinhão, a fruit of the local araucaria trees, and gives the houses an organic sinuous form. The elliptical plan of the social level that contains an indoor SPA with swimming pool and sauna is very fluid and defines the built volume of the house. The social level is reached via a ramp, instead of stairs, that dims the light towards the most introspective space in the house, the wine cellar. The entrance hall provides the opposite experience for those ascending the ramp towards the living room. Above the social level, there are four suites and a home office with 180 degrees views of the surrounding mountains and native araucaria trees.

Campos do Jordão

c

d

a
The large glass windows transform the ramp path between the living room and the upper floor into a pleasant walk with a view.

b
The large roof rises above the house and points to the sky.

c
The route through the house is made through spaces that open and contract.

d
Wood and stone provide the warmth desired by the owners.

e
The swimming pool along the curved wall.

f
Section and floor plans.

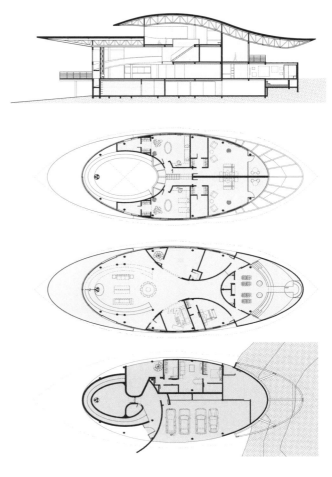

# Monolocale
# Effe

Interior design
Archiplanstudio

Location
Via Calvi, 46100 Mantua,
Italy

Year
2021

Gross floor area
36 m²

Number of bedrooms
1

The architects' approach was guided by the small dimensions and the peculiarity of walls decoration, frescoes from the 15th and 19th centuries, which were found during the work on site. In order to preserve and enhance this special situation, the architects realized a small wooden volume in which the bed is located. The volume fits into the unified interior space of the apartment and defines its own hierarchy and path. In the bedroom, detached from the ceiling and the walls, the mattress on the floor and some shelves on one wall are the essential elements. In the living area, simple furnishings designed by the architects create a familiar situation. Each element allows to create an essential house, where only the kitchen has a different material definition, with doors in brass laminate.

Mantua

e

f

g

a
View of the spacious apartment, where historical frescos meet contemporary interior design.

b
The noble and simple bathroom visually matches the kitchen.

c
The walls configure a bacterial view of the object, in which time's decay has his own value.

d
The small box shows some selective openings that allow visual relationships with the surrounding space.

e
An open wardrobe is placed opposite the bed.

f
Minimalist wooden furniture emphasizes the original walls.

g
Ground floor plan.

# Onyx Moon Loft
## Prague

Interior design and architecture
a1 architects

Location
Prague,
Czech Republic

Year
2017

Gross floor area
220 m²

Number of bedrooms
2

The apartment is filled with unique details as well as niches and small corners where residents can place flowers. Two motifs are reflected in the apartment: the magnificent view of the castle and the owner's passion for onyx. Therefore, an onyx moon was integrated into the bedroom. The stone symbolizes tranquility and eternity and contrasts with the lively panorama of the castle and the river, which can be observed through the large window. The original disposition of the apartment, the connections, the visual axes, the openings and the furniture are simplified and purified. Most of the metalwork was done in brass. All door knobs and handles for the furniture were designed in collaboration with Klára Šumová. The glass fillings for the door handles and the door knobs were made by Czech glassblowers. The chandeliers were designed by the studio Dechem and the unique illustrations on the heating screens and walls were painted by Michal Bačák.

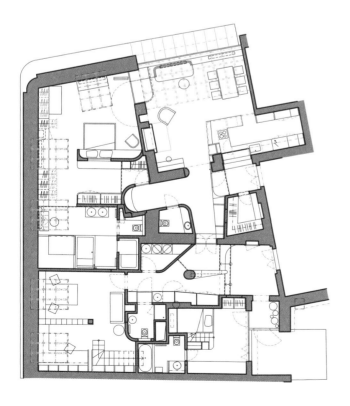

d

e

f

a

A large window front allows an exceptional view of the old town.

b

The interior design of the kitchen appears calm and modern and invites to a relaxed cooking.

c

Above the bed an onyx moon is placed, which creates a calm atmosphere in the sleeping area.

d

The glass fillings of the hand knobs were designed by Klára Šumová and handmade by Czech glass-blowers.

e

Green plants bring life into the noble bathroom.

f

Floor plan.

# El
# Patio

Interior design
Malluvia Innenarchitektur

Location
Sendling/Westpark, Munich,
Germany

Year
2020

Gross floor area
463,2 m²

Number of bedrooms
2

In the heart of Munich, a 1950s warehouse that most recently served as a photo studio was completely redefined. During the initial remodeling ten years ago, a room-in-room cube with sanitary areas was installed. This had to be integrated into the new design. Cross-room style elements such as dark-stained slats with brass caps take up the structure of the existing cube and are reflected in the bedroom. Fixed glazing placed directly in front of the bed provides a view throughout the room. The glazing can be turned milky at the touch of a button to maintain privacy in the bedroom as well. The black lacquered trims and window elements contrast with the dark stained, French, herringbone pattern and the filigree coffers on the furniture fronts.

## Munich

a
General view of kitchen, dining, and living.

b
The living room wall seamlessly merges with kitchen.

c
Dining and kitchen with the remodeled cube behind the table.

d
Children's room with pull out boxes under the bench.

e
Sections and floor plan.

f
Jacuzzi recessed in the cavity floor.

g
The existing cube was integrated by color and the repeating slats.

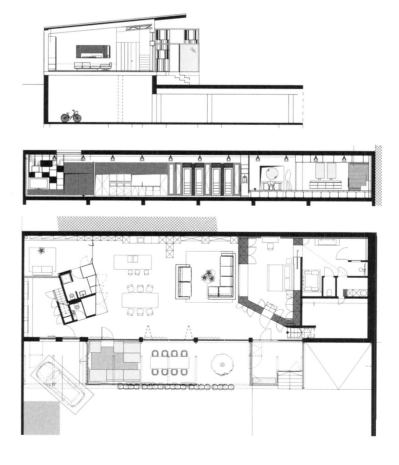

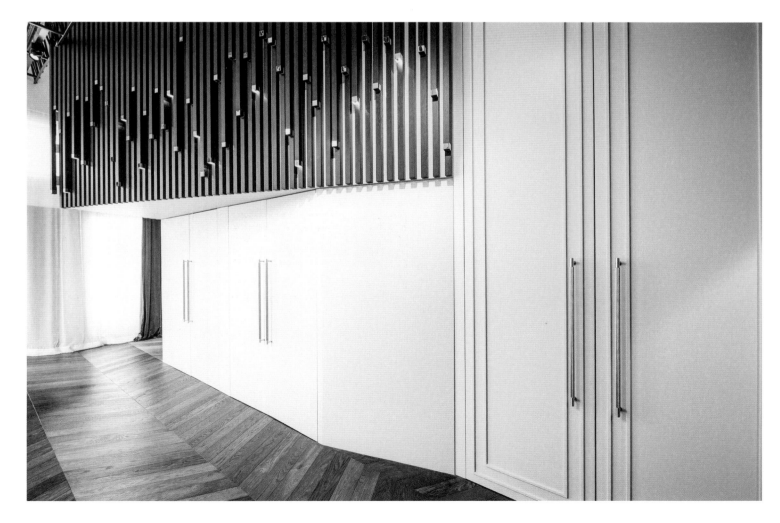

# Library Home
## Shanghai

Interior design
atelier tao+c

Architecture
László Hudec

Location
1850 Huaihai Road, Xuhui District,
Shanghai

Year
2017

Gross floor area
95 m²

Number of bedrooms
1

The architects were commissioned to renovate a small apartment on the top floor of the International Savings Society Apartments, one of the earliest high-rise residential apartment buildings in Shanghai. The existing structures and concrete façade were preserved and exposed while all interior partitions were demolished, creating an open design walls that removes the boundaries between rooms. The architects placed a dominant oak bookshelf that extends from floor to ceiling. The bedroom and living room are arranged around and below the bookshelves and merging seamlessly. In response to the diagonal line of the bookshelves and the building envelope, a small elevated attic along the corner was introduced to break up the homogeneous space of a one level apartment. A narrow staircase leads to a small mezzanine level. Surrounded by the bookshelves, a space inhabited by books, objects and people was created, characterized by serenity.

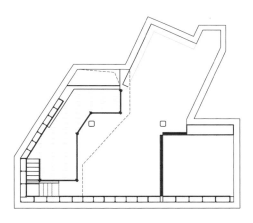

a
Ceiling-high bookshelves, open spaces and a mezzanine level characterize the apartment.

b
Seamless transition of living and sleeping area makes the apartment appear bright and spacious.

c
Since the concrete beams are visible, it feels as if one is under the protection of a roof.

d
In the noble bathroom classic materials contrast with modern interior design.

e
A narrow staircase leads to the mezzanine level of the apartment.

f
Mezzanine floor and floor plan.

# Wood House

Interior design and architecture
Neugebauer Architekten

Location
Riederbergstraße 78,
65195 Wiesbaden,
Germany

Year
2019

Gross floor area
430 m²

Number of bedrooms
5

The goal of the project was to design a building biologically sound, low-tech single family house made of solid wood for a family of five to live, reside and work in. The floor plan thrives on the combination of open living and defined spaces without losing its coziness. There are no classic hallways, but rooms that can be used as places to gather. On the first floor, the three children have their places of retreat, and in the hallway or play zone, everyone can come together. The top floor is the parents' area with a large office with two home office workstations, and the hallway provides space for the fitness workout. Lots of built-in cabinets across the floors keep everything organized. The basement has room for guests to stay overnight, and there is a dirt floor and sand pit under the garage.

Wiesbaden

a
The open ground floor with a smooth transition to the outside can be used for coming together.

b
The large roof overhangs protect the façade from the weather.

c
In the bright, spacious kitchen one can cook with a view of the garden.

d
Ground floor plan and cross section.

e
Built-in cupboards on the three floors provide the necessary order.

f
The bedroom is located in the north and darkkept for an optimal sleeping climate.

g
The tilted roof with a round ridge creates high rooms inside with few roof slopes.

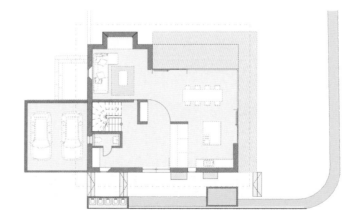

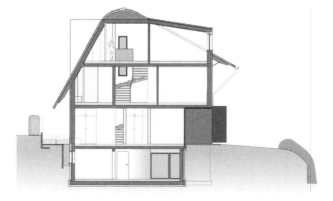

# In Perfect Harmony

a

**Interior design**
herzog, kassel + partner

**Location**
Karlsruhe,
Germany

**Year**
2018

**Gross floor area**
220 m²

**Number of bedrooms**
2

In this high-quality residential property two large attic apartments were combined to form an airy maisonette. The client asked for a noble but also as comfortable as possible refuge, that meets all functional requirements and yet visually preserves the character of the old building. The most modern technical equipment should be present, but not visible. Instead, the old character of the building serves as an essential design element. The upper floor contains an open kitchen-dining-living area. The central box is the connecting element between the two parts of the room, designed as multifunctional furniture and room divider. This gives the occupants a feeling of pleasant security despite the openness and size of the floor.

## Karlsruhe

a
The harmonious color concept in combination with the lighting design makes it possible to create atmospheric scenarios.

b
The old exposed brick wall expresses the old character of the building.

c
The kitchen receives its unique look through the different materials and the smooth, sleek finish.

d
Ground floor plan.

e
The multifunctional room divider also accommodates the wardrobe, technology and storage space.

# Wohnung 1625
## Munich

Interior design
von Moltke InnenArchitekten

Location
Munich, Germany

Year
2018

Gross floor area
120 m²

Number of bedrooms
3

Untouched since the 1960s, this bright and clean maisonette eventually could not withstand the everyday family life of its new owners. The cramped and dark impression of the former apartment was resolved by targeted interventions in the building fabric and a sophisticated light concept. By enlarging the bathrooms, a passageway became the longed-for children's room and space was created for a guest bathroom. Openings into adjacent rooms and glass elements allow daylight to flood the rooms and provide a view from the hallway into the living and dining area outside the window. LED strips and compartments for decorative lights integrated in the custom-made furniture are complemented by accentuating spots and atmospheric lights. The color white, combined with powdery pastel tones and wood, dominates the apartment. This creates a coziness which is always light and allows the newly won space to breathe.

d

e

f

a
The large white surfaces of the bookshelf and light chairs contribute to the spaciousness of the dining area.

b
The green color of the sofa harmonizes with the warm brown of the wooden floor.

c
The eye-catching staircase is gleaming white with dark brown wood inserts and a matching hand-rail.

d
Spotlights facing the wardrobe and LED strips inside makes dressing in the morning a special experience.

e
In the bathroom, warm blue wall elements, pow-dery pink tiles and a wooden washstand alternate with accents of white.

f
First floor plan.

# Kandilli House

a

Interior design
ofist

Location
Kandilli, Istanbul,
Turkey

Year
2019

Gross floor area
100 m²

Number of bedrooms
1

Kandilli House is a cozy little home in a pleasant garden facing the beautiful Bosphorus, designed for a young man, who avoids social media and almost every smartphone-app, although owning a successful tech business. Originally from a Mediterranean village, he still spends all his vacations back home where he grew up and enjoys the peacefulness of the raw, primitive life. Between two chaotic metropolises like Istanbul and London, this little house is designed as a synthesis of a village and a city house. It is designed for just the basic needs of life – very functional and just enough. Nestling over Bosphorus, the traditional feelings, local textures, fabrics and habits act as the main characteristic of the house, where as the base design is sleek and modern, since living and working in the middle of the busy city requires a modern and practical living.

## Istanbul

d

e

f

a

Dark colors in the bedroom create a relaxing and cozy atmosphere while the wall-high windows offer a constant connection to nature.

b

Wild and colorful patterns give the living room an unique look.

c

In the inviting living room provides a pleasant atmosphere for making music and relax.

d

The colorful combination of tiles and carpet with wooden elements make the bathroom very cozy.

e

The garden's pavilion with it's bright orange chairs picks up the colorful palette on the inside.

f

Ground floor plan.

# HV
# Pavillon

a

Interior design and architecture
GGA gardini gibertini architects

Location
Castel del Piano,
Italy

Year
2021

Gross floor area
230 m²

Number of bedrooms
3

The HV Pavilion is located in the foothills of Mount Amiata in the Tuscan Maremma. As a proscenium, the typical Mediterranean residence opens theatrically into the landscape. The rooms are arranged around the central courtyard with Roman-Italian reminiscences. The floor is made of cement resin and has the color of sunburnt grass. Natural wood completes the spaces. A steel kitchen island and a cast cement table celebrate the rite of Italian cooking and emphasize the convivial character of the house. The furnishings are a spatial continuum between the fireplace and the olive grove. The geometry on the outside honors the local building tradition of dry stone walls and the wooden infills recall the closing elements of the rural buildings of the Amiatini. In this way, the building merges with the landscape and ties it into its own history.

Castel del Piano

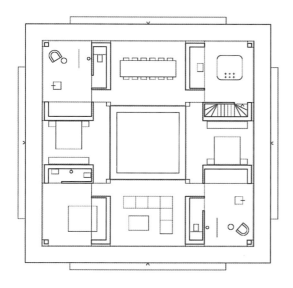

# Family Living

Interior design
Gabriela Raible Innenarchitektur
Planungsgesellschaft

Architecture
Harder Groh Architekten

Location
Munich,
Germany

Year
2020

Gross floor area
220 m²

Number of bedrooms
4

Intelligent spatial structures, a clear design language and modern lines characterize the project for a family with two small children in a semi-detached house. The house measures 220 square meters of floor space and is located in the Bogenhausen district of Munich. It clearly shows the designer's signature: Together with her project manager Maren Boettcher, she implemented a modern, imaginative and sophisticated interior concept with numerous fine details. The  house itself was planned by Munich-based Harder Groh Architekten and features floor-to-ceiling windows and a generous dormer window. The design of the semi-detached house is minimalist and very homely at the same time. All areas are open and flooded with light. The tunnel fireplace at floor level in the hallway area provides exciting views across the living room and into the garden.

Munich

d

a
The marble design of the kitchen gives it a clean and modern look.

b
Ball-shaped lamps and blue chairs add color to the open dining area.

c
The living room offers enough seating options for the occupants and possible visitors.

d
The living area is flooded with light and touches of color add a feeling of coziness and warmth.

e
Ground floor plan.

e

# framed

Interior design and architecture
fabi architekten

Location
Traunstein,
Germany

Year
2020

Gross floor area
435 m²

Number of bedrooms
4

The property blends in with the surrounding Chiemgau Alps through its elevated hillside location. The volume is structured by materials. The wood-clad upper floor hosts the entrance and living level. The spacious, airy gable roof structure cantilevers over the garden level. It faces the Chiemgau Alps and, through large, purposefully placed window openings, brings the surroundings directly into the house. This effect is enhanced by a seemingly floating loggia section, which is extended by a cantilevered platform. Thus, the view has an immediate effect on the viewer. The lower garden level hosts private and some ancillary rooms. This recessed floor level is set off by a dark gray façade and forms a quiet, comfortable background for the garden terrace and a covered opens pace.

## Traunstein

a
Bright-colored eyecatchers are play-
fully positioned in the natural-colored
interior of the dining and living area.

b
The loggia offers a view across the
Chiemgau Alps.

c
Elegant black-and-white contrasts
combined with wooden elements and
gray tiles fill the master bathroom with
a warm atmosphere.

d
First floor plan.

e
The single-flight staircase is located
at the slope side and completely lit by
daylight through a void.

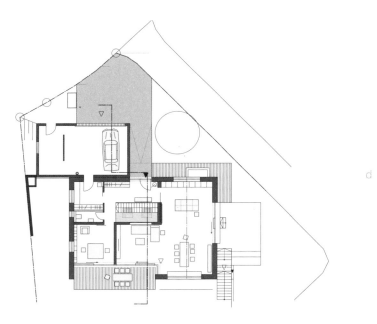

# Langham Nymphenburg Residence

a

**Interior design**
MangMauritz

**Location**
Nymphenburg, Munich,
Germany

**Year**
2020

**Gross floor area**
836 m²

**Number of bedrooms**
4

The intimate domicile in a more than 200-year-old cavalier's
house of Nymphenburg Palace combines the amenities of
a five-star hotel with the fairy-tale flair of a private
18th-century castle – and the incomparable aura of the fine
objects especially made for the interior in the adjacent porcelain manufactory. The manufactory's guest house is not only
a luxurious hostel at the interface between town and country,
but also a showcase for the many possible applications of objects made of Nymphenburg porcelain. MangMauritz retained
the stately character of the building, but also lent it a great
sense of homeliness through the use of wallpaper and textiles.
They integrated four bedrooms, three lounges, a kitchen and
seven bathrooms into the generous room layout.

## Munich

d

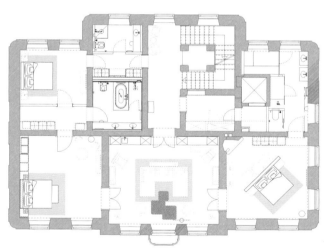

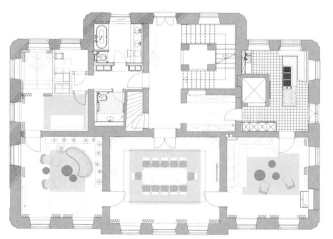

a

The generous seating landscape with throw pillows in Jim Thompson fabrics fully embraces the home's urban connection.

b

The dining area with its palette of gray and exotic touch, nature and urban space merge once again through porcelain pieces that depict natural objects.

c

Seating with a wall of objects from Porzellan Manufaktur Nymphenburg.

d

Warm toned colors in the ladies room create a cozy atmosphere while golden elements lend it a high-quality finish.

e

Detail of the filigree patterns in the bedroom.

f

The bedroom showcases porcelain objects from Porzellan Manufaktur Nymphenburg.

g

First floor and ground floor plan.

# Cordero
# Residence

Interior design and architecture
tang kawasaki studio

Location
New York City, NY,
USA

Year
2017

Gross floor area
650 m²

Number of bedrooms
1

This home overlooking Central Park West is a sanctuary in the city for meditation and restoration. Instead of creating an active space that promotes hybrid uses of a small living space to replicate the functions of larger homes, the agenda was to create a passive living space which relied on a dialogue between designer and end-user to define a discrete, empathetic program for the quartet of spaces. Inspired by guest houses in Kyoto a sequence of modest spaces with a minimalist palette was created. Materials were selected through a lens of reflection on the reductive characteristics of comfort – visually and tactilely. Waxed European oak, Bateig limestone, bronze-glazed ceramics, and Calacatta marble are balanced against Merino wool felt and Igusa tatami.

# New York City

a
The dark, reflecting brick wall in the kitchen gives it a clean and modern look.

b
The living room and sleeping room area are separated by a closet to make optimal use of the small space.

c
The kitchen windows offer a generous view over New York's Central Park.

d
The sleeping area further functions as a dressing room.

e
Ground floor plan and cross section.

f
The spacious living room is flooded with light.

# Casa AP

## Zapopan

Interior design
Colectivo Sur

Architecture
Elías Rizo Arquitectos

Location
Zapopan,
Mexico

Year
2018

Gross floor area
2.748 m²

Number of bedrooms
6

Designed in a private subdivision for a young family, Casa AP is a project marked by dualities throughout. The house is separated into two volumes, one public and the other private, connected by a lobby that joins an exterior reflecting pool to the interior that leads to a rear garden to guide users to the private or public area. The design intended to bring occupants into constant contact with the outdoors while maintaining their privacy at all times; the house is blind to the street while the east-facing public area opens up almost completely to the rear garden and partially to the reflecting pool that adjoins the lobby, on the central axis. The stone structures give visual and solar protection on the southern façade that has the street frontage. Despite the house's large size, it was given the cozy feel of a smaller home that creates a feeling of intimacy and helps foster easy interactions among its occupants.

a
The exterior pool-area between the separated house volumes.

b
Dark colours create a feeling of coziness and intimacy inside the living room which is flooded with light.

c
The connecting lobby as the central meeting point leads to all the different areas.

d
Ground floor plan.

e
The panoramic windows allow the occupants to permanently stay in contact with nature.

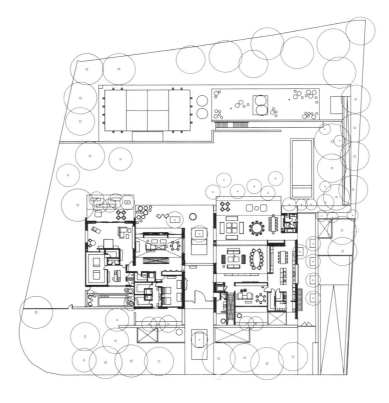

d

# House by the Bailucchi

**Interior design and architecture**
llabb architettura

**Location**
Piazza di Santa Maria
in Passione 28/11, Genova,
Italy

**Year**
2020

**Gross floor area**
135 m²

**Number of bedrooms**
2

Flooded with light reflected from the sea, this apartment fits into the intimacy of the neighborhood. The apartment is on two floors, the merging of two distinct units of which the one on the upper floor is undoubtedly the most interesting. The entrance is on the lower floor, where the sleeping quarters are located. Connecting the two levels was the biggest challenge; the space was small and the level difference was substantial. A couple of steps lead to a concrete platform. From here a light metal structure winds its way up to the upper floor. The apartment, in all its complexity, is dotted with works of art. The entire living area overlooks the long terrace. A dialogue between interior and exterior that sets this renovation in the framework of a lively and confident reflection on the city is created.

## Genova

d

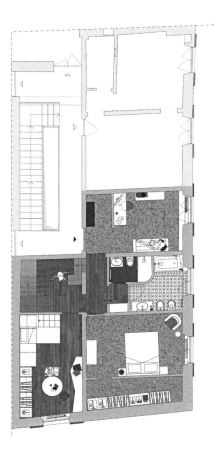

a
The artwork and special details make the apartment feel like a cross between a home and a small inhabited gallery.

b
The living area overlooks the long terrace while large windows floods the inside with natural light.

c
The oak staircase with its light metal structure and a blue nautical rope railing winds its way to the upper floor.

d
The bright dining area with its colorful accents invites to cook and get together.

e
Ground floor plan.

# Lightweight Concrete House

a

**Interior design and architecture**
baurmann.dürr architekten

**Location**
Ettlingen,
Germany

**Year**
2019

**Gross floor area**
410 m²

**Number of bedrooms**
4

The single-family house is monolithically constructed, with solid exterior walls of lightweight concrete, which becomes the aesthetic expression of the whole building. The interior walls contrast with the load-bearing exterior walls, as they are conventionally masonry, plastered with lime and painted white. The kitchen and dining area are located on the upper floor, it is joined by a large roof terrace with outdoor fireplace to stage the panoramic view. The living room with access to the garden and the master bedroom are located on the garden floor, while the entrance and other private rooms are on the ground floor. The three floors are connected by a single flight staircase and through an air space.

Ettlingen

e

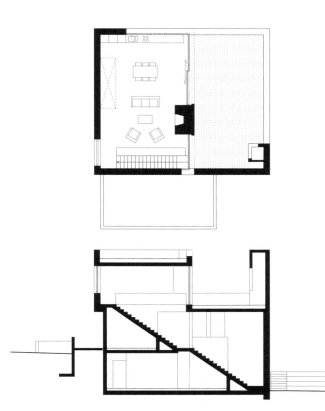

f

a
The velvety concrete surface of the exterior wall also characterizes the interior.

b
Since the view can only be experienced on the upper floor, the dining room is located there.

c
The spacious dining room is adjoined by the roof terrace with an outdoor fireplace, which creates a cozy outdoor space at any time of the year.

d
A single flight staircase and an air space create a connection between the floors.

e
The lightweight concrete is neither plastered nor painted and thus defines the colorfulness of the exterior walls.

f
Upper floor plan and cross section.

# Beyond

## Cape Town

Interior design
ARRCC

Architecture
SAOTA

Location
Nettleton Road, Cape Town,
South Africa

Year
2018

Gross floor area
1400 m²

Number of bedrooms
6

Beyond is a contemporary setting for life and art, where the full comfort of a modern home is potently married to an elemental architecture drawn from its dramatic setting. The lower levels play host to six generous bedrooms, three of which can be interlinked for a family suite, and to a double volume entertainment space complete with spa, games and cinema. Principal living is at the very top of the building – an expansive, double-height open plan space which houses kitchen, bar, dining, living and family rooms as well as a winter lounge, study and art studio at a mezzanine level. From the cavernous entrance hall the visitor is led upwards towards the generous light of the upper living levels. The masterful interplay of light, space and raw materiality in the house plays generous host to its other family – a considered collection of contemporary South African art. The interior was designed by ARRCC, the bespoke furniture by OKHA.

a
Cinema and games room with Blowfish by Porky Hefer and a Cecil Skotnes tapestry.

b
The pool overlooking the landscape.

c
Main bedroom with a Bird chair by Harry Bertoia and Jada couch by OKHA, over the Flokati rug. Carnival artwork by Yvon van der Heul.

d
First and second floor plan.

e
Double volume entrance foyer with Totem by David Brown and steel wall sculpture by Paul Edmunds.

f
Family room with double volume tapestry is by the Keiskama Trust, Andrzej Urbanski landscape artwork and artwork adjacent is Nzuri Fufu by Cyrus Kabiru.

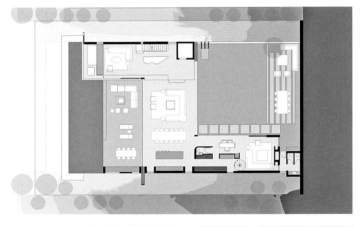

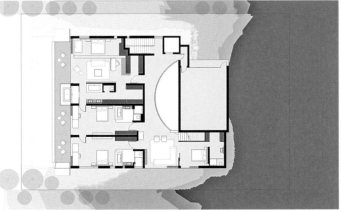

# Penthouse
# Salzburg

Interior design and architecture
Bernd Gruber Kitzbühel

Location
Salzburg,
Austria

Year
2019

Gross floor area
202 m²

Number of bedrooms
1

Realizing one's own demands in one's own project without compromises is one of the greatest challenges of an interior designer. The designers of Penthouse Salzburg met this challenge with their two story domicile. Coziness, timelessness and an uncompromising demand for function were the most important guiding principles for this project. The personal art collection and the recurring warm colors on the walls and in the furniture create an inviting atmosphere. The barely visible storage spaces were unobtrusively integrated into the room structure. Contrary to some conventions, the ceilings are clad in wood and the floor has a concrete look. This object shows how traditional craftsmanship and contemporary interior design merge into a harmonious overall picture.

a
The spacious master bathroom showcases pieces of the designers' personal art collection.

b
A dark blue moon above the bath tub forms an eyecatcher.

c
In the dressing room, wooden wardrobes with glass doors are set in an elegant light.

d
A warm blue wall adds to the coziness of the living room.

e
Quiet dominant gray blends kitchen and living-space.

f
First floor plan.

# Shire
# House

a

Interior design and architecture
Graham Jones Design

Location
Mornington Peninsula, Victoria,
Australia

Year
2015

Gross floor area
900 m²

Number of bedrooms
5

Shire House on Melbourne's Mornington Peninsula has been crafted to accommodate and enhance active and family-oriented beachfront living. A perfect marriage of design, attention to detail and quality finish. The front entry and façade are striking yet understated, whilst inside the visitor meets open, flowing and naturally lit spaces that offer constant connection between family members and sweeping views of the water. A large, roofed upper terrace appears to float as it runs the full length of the home, whilst an expansive tiled alfresco invites you to relax beside the wet-edge pool, perched three meters above the ground and surrounded by manicured grounds complete with a tennis court – a breathtaking family home that makes every day feel like being on holiday.

# Victoria

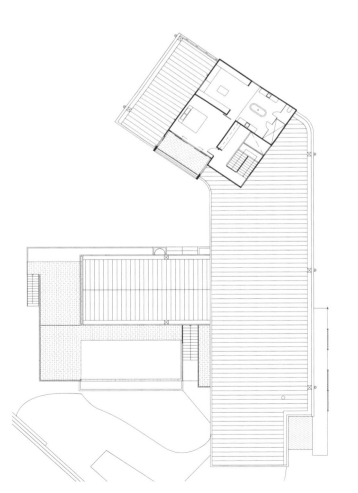

a
Waves on turquoise on the walls bring the ocean into the en-suite bathroom.

b
Gray kitchen joinery adds particular shine to the house.

c
The kitchen adjoins the open plan living space.

d
Second floor plan.

e
The living space opens onto the terrace.

# Kids Haven
## Zurich

Interior design and architecture
Collab Interiors

Location
Near Zurich,
Switzerland

Year
2020

Gross floor area
530 m²

Number of bedrooms
4

A 20-year-old home has been remodeled for a family with two children. The focus entirely lies on the children and their wishes. By that it was possible to incorporate unique elements like a slide connecting entrance and playroom. The playroom includes a climbing wall, a tree house, a painting corner, a swing and even a beanbag hanging from the ceiling. There is plenty of space to play, create and have fun. The children's bedroom was also specially designed for the two little girls. An unicorn wallpaper, their favorite color on the walls and even a tipi with comfortable pillows were included. The absolute highlight of the bedroom is the large wooden tree with birds which disguises the existing fireplace pipe, creating a dreamy oasis. Not only the latest additions but also the complete basic construction for all other rooms were planned and built by Collab Interiors.

a
The neutral colors in the living room combined with playful items, create a calm yet fun atmosphere.

b
The new slide for young and old connecting entrance and family play room.

c
Play and reading area with tipi and wooden tree in the girl's bedroom.

d
Second floor plan.

e
Sleeping area with included unicorn wallpaper, adapted to the girl's wishes.

f
Light flooded play room with multiple activities and animal parade wallpaper.

# City
# Apartment

Interior design
Sebastian Zenker

Location
Bogenhausen, Munich,
Germany

Year
2019

Gross floor area
230 m²

Number of bedrooms
4

This modern home is located in the Bogenhausen district of Munich and offers plenty of space for its residents, a family with two children, by combining two apartments. The clients wanted an elegant and casual city apartment, whose furnishings should result in an exciting mix of mid-century, pop colorband high-quality fixtures in combination with classic elements and exquisite furniture. Real wood parquet flooring, contrasting wall colors and built-in cabinets from Holzrausch Planung Manufaktur form the basis of the apartment. Characterful vintage and custom pieces meet design must-haves such as lights by Occhio, seating by Meridiani or rugs by Tai Ping. The utility room is the highlight of the apartment. The bright yellow color gives the room a very special effect.

## Munich

a
Noble designer products characterize the apartment.

b
A coherent color concept and contrasting details and accessories make for an exciting composition.

c
The wall at the end of the corridor reprises the bedrooms colors.

d
The utility room in bright yellow is defined by a purist design language and functionality.

e
Dark furniture harmonize with the light-flooded kitchen.

f
Ground floor plan.

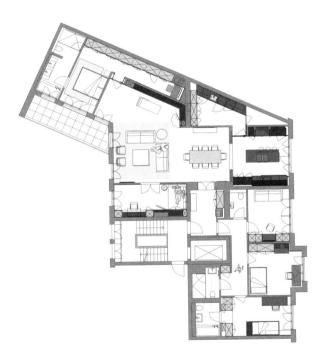

# House
# Sandfeld

Interior design and architecture
baurmann.dürr architekten

Location
Karlsruhe,
Germany

Year
2020

Gross floor area
345 m²

Number of bedrooms
4

The simple residential house lives from its inner and outer space formation. The positioning on the plot with the angular carport creates an entrance courtyard for the playing children, while the house garden is protected thanks to the transverse construction. Inside, the dining area forms the center around which the individual functional areas are arranged. A two-flight wooden staircase leads to the more private upper floor with the three children's bedrooms and the parents' wing. The decision not to build a basement results in larger storage areas on the ground floor and space for the building services in the carport extension.

Karlsruhe

a
Large windows flood the house with light.

b
The dining room with a large table is the center of the house and provides space for the family to get together.

c
The two-flight wooden staircase leads to the upper floor with the bedroom and children's rooms.

d
The terrace and garden are located behind the house and thus provide a private space.

e
First and ground floor plan.

# La Loica and
# La Tagua

Interior design and architecture
Croxatto & Opazo Arquitectos

Location
Camino a Lagunillas, Matanzas, Navidad,
Chile

Year
2018

Gross floor area
19 m² + 24 m²

Number of bedrooms
1 + 1

This Project was born as a holiday home on the coast. The two cabins for two people each, are placed 80 meters above sea level on the Lagunilla hill and rise in front of the Lobera, a large rock mass jutting out of the sea. Matanzas has become a world capital for Windsurfing and Kitesurfing, thanks to its outstanding wind and wave conditions. Both these elements were purposefully incorporated into the development of the project. The design process was conceived as an opportunity for experimentation, looking for a way to both dominate and blend-in with the surrounding nature. "La Loica" and "La Tagua", both named after bird species native to the region, are placed on the ravine using a wooden structure that supports the main platform, over which the program is developed.

Matanzas

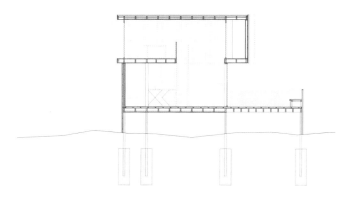

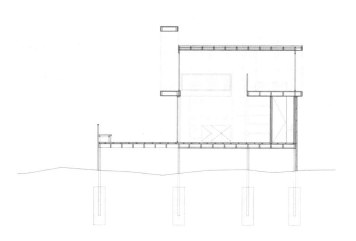

a
Both buildings are built entirely in wood, using impregnated, chamber-dried pine on the main structures.

b
A loft connects the interior premises both visually and spatially.

c
The dining room, bathroom and kitchen are laid out on the access level using furniture that merges with the architecture.

d
La Loica and La Tagua cross section.

e
Large windows enhance the feeling of hovering over the ocean while a connection between interior and exterior is created.

# Maxvorstadt Roof

Interior design
Unterlandstättner Architekten

Location
Munich,
Germany

Year
2020

Gross floor area
372.5 m²

Number of bedrooms
2

This spacious new construction of an attic apartment on an old Munich building was designed as a rental apartment, including bathroom and kitchen facilities. The roof space on the top floor extends over the entire width of the house and offers a spacious living, cooking, dining area with two roof terraces, to the east and to the west. The early inclusion of the planning of built-in furniture was an elementary part of the design process and reinforces the spaciousness by the choice of materials and integration into the spatial structure. The oversized, largely frameless skylights and the roof terraces open up unexpected perspectives with views over the roofs of Munich in the dense inner-city environment of Maxvorstadt all the way to the Alps.

Munich

a
Spaciousness by the choice of materials and purified lines.

b
Built-in furniture is part of the entire interior.

c
Views across Munich's Maxvorstadt provide spaciousness and urbanity.

d
Ground floor and first floor plan.

e
Oversized, largely frameless skylights flood the rooms with light.

d

# CLT
# House

Interior design and architecture
FMD Architects

Location
Victoria,
Australia

Year
2019

Gross floor area
560 m²

Number of bedrooms
7

CLT House is a bridge between architectural thinking and sustainable construction methods. It is a poetic and pragmatic balance between architect and builder, whose relationship developed from the concept design to ensure a highly considered outcome. From the outset the house was designed with cross laminated timber, CLT. This is celebrated by exposing the structure throughout, demanding absolute precision in the construction system. Typical daily experiences are elevated beyond ritual to full immersion with nature, the timber interior bringing a constant calm and soothing experience. The large multi-purpose bridge serves as a quiet retreat for the owners, its central location, which spans the different wings of the house, allows all three generations to come together.

## Victoria

a
The minimalistic timber interior brings a constant calm and soothing experience.

b
Interior elements are also made from timber to emphasize the natural qualities of the materials.

c
Wall high windows allow a constant immersion with nature in every room.

d
Cross section and ground floor plan.

e
The rhythmic sawtooth roof integrates an extensive solar array with high level windows.

f
The kitchen acts as an pivot point between the existing section and the new CLT extension.

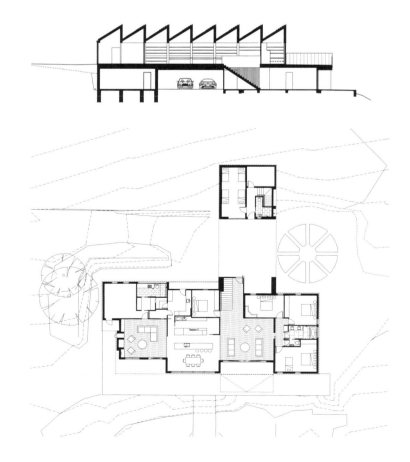

# A Designer
# Home

Interior design
Einat Shahar Design studio

Architecture
Ruth Eliezer Architect

Location
62 Harimon Street, Kfar Harif, 7983000,
Israel

Year
2020

Gross floor area
140 m²

Number of bedrooms
2-3

The designer's own home is a one-story wooden house with high ceilings carried by wooden beams. It features large sliding windows inviting natural light into the house and blurring the boundaries between the inside and outside. A terrace along the house merges into the large garden with a beautiful vine arbor. The mezzanine above the dining space allows an open family room. The house is spacious and minimalist with natural materials and a soft color pallet. The woodwork pieces were designed by the owner and handcrafted by her spouse, an avid woodworker with great attention to detail. The furniture was carefully selected. The combination of materials and textures creates a unique layered look that characterizes the designer vision for a warm, homey feeling.

## Kfar Harif

a
The minimalist but chic interior ac-
centuates the calm character of the
building.

b
The spacious dining room is flooded
with daylight and offers enough room
for visitors.

c
Wooden elements in the kitchen
match the wooden beams of the
ceiling.

d
Ground floor plan.

e
The living room with its high ceilings
and large windows invites natural light
from the outside.

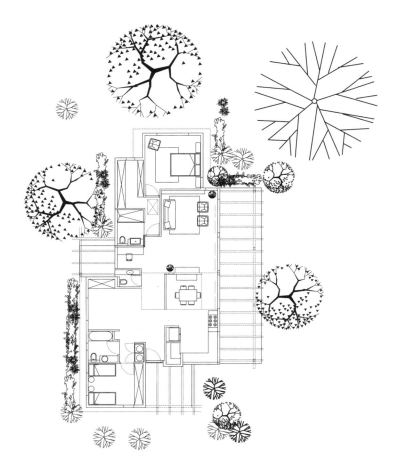

# Orchard House

Interior design and architecture
Dada Partners

Location
Chattarpur, New Dehli,
India

Year
2018

Gross floor area
930 m²

Number of bedrooms
6

Set in a dense grid of mature mango trees, the project reflects the dichotomy of respecting the territory belonging to the tree trunks while inscribing our own rhythm on the ground. While the property is 4.000 square meters large, the building is firmly set towards the south-west corner. By that the rest of the orchard could be preserved as a permanent green. A series of stone clad walls are used as design tool to spatially define the three courts and to engage directly with the building. Viewed from the open courts these walls – as if acting like a folly – manage to extend the built experience and elude any clear understanding of the buildings scale or extent. A consistent tectonic of steel, timber, glass, and stone, along with gray colored walls seem nestled within the deep colored trunks and leaves of the orchard. Sleek pivoted wooden louvered screens along the bedroom-terraces provide a sense of privacy and help filter the summer sun.

New Dehli

a
The design emerges from a balancing act between layout and composition.

b
Glass, curtains, and wooden shutters are the main kind of walls.

c
A linear staircase ascends a double height sunlight space.

d
One of the two bedrooms ends in terraces that seem to project into the landscape.

e
Ground floor plan and cross section.

f
The intimate entry portico with the front door.

g
A consistent tectonic of steel along with gray colored walls.

h
The pool court along the stone walls was designed around the trees.

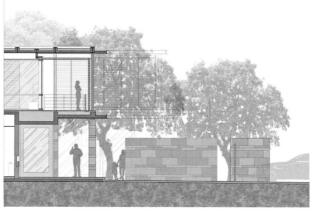

f

g

h

# House
# G 16

Interior design and architecture
Architekturbüro Markus Mucha

Location
near Heidelberg,
Germany

Year
2016

Gross floor area
505 m²

Number of bedrooms
3

In the spirit of classical modernism, this single-family house is characterized by its clear design language and its careful integration into the generous hillside plot. The building is accessed via basement, which is embedded in the slope. For economic reasons, the office, garage and ancillary rooms are located here. A stair tower forms the access to the living level. The interior presents itself in a simple contrast of white and oak. The main floor floats above the garden. It is divided into three spaces: the central dining area separates the two sleeping areas for children and parents. The large windows with their oak profiles frame the surrounding landscape. The covered terrace forms the transition between the garden and the interior. Rich colors on the inside emphasize the private rooms.

Heidelberg

d

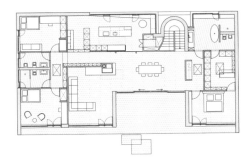

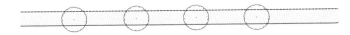

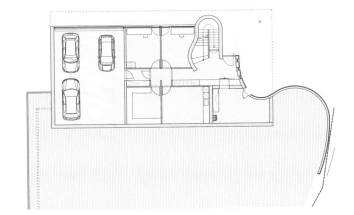

a
Dining room in elegant simplicity.

b
Bathtub with a view.

c
Different white surface and oak predominate the interior.

d
On the garden side the upper floor looks like a bungalow.

e
Ground and first floor plan.

# Mo-tel
# House

a

interior design
Office S&M

Location
Islington, London,
United Kingdom

Year
2020

Gross floor area
60 m² (ground floor)

Mo-tel House is a remodeling of the lower ground floor of a Victorian townhouse in Islington, London, for a young family of four by London-based Office S&M. The interior uses color to striking effect and its designers chose materials with a previous existence and a story to tell. The suite of robust furniture pieces, each designed to be as much a small piece of architecture as an item of furniture or a building in a city, creates a series of interconnected but distinct spaces. Each piece of furniture serves more than one function: A pink and blue bench with crested canopy acts as dining seating, cozy reading nook, storage, regal throne, and cabinet to display curiosities collected during the family's travels. This allows each family member to find new uses for the furniture.

## London

b

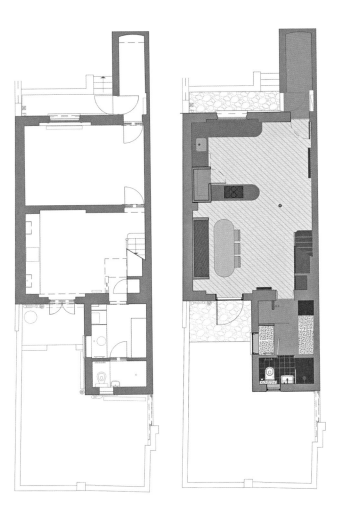

a
The pink bench enclosure with blue upholstered cushions for the family to nestle and relax.

b
Cupboards beneath the stair are painted in a deep blue with circular red finger pulls.

c
A blue curved kitchen larder with a projecting 'nose' which illuminates the worktop and a mirrored eye that winks each time you open the door.

d
Shower room and WC which is accessed via the utility room.

e
Bathroom: the luxurious marbled worktops by Smile Plastics re-uses melted, discarded milk bottles and chopping boards.

f
Ground floor plan before and after.

# South
# Villa

Interior design
ARRCC

Interior Decor
OKHA

Architecture
SAOTA

Location
Clifton, Cape Town,
South Africa

Year
2019

Gross floor area
958.4 m²

Number of bedrooms
5

ARRCC and OKHA have established stylistic connections to the style modern movement of the Art Deco period of the 1920s and 30s in these apartments. Each apartment effortlessly binds state-of-the-art technologies into the fabric of its functionality and existence with 24/7 security, services, and amenities that afford a lock-up-and-go lifestyle for summer or all-year-round living. The penthouse doubles as a private art gallery, curated by OKHA in collaboration with the client. There is a broad range of custom-designed OKHA furniture pieces featured in key areas throughout the apartment. Taking their cue from the architecture, OKHA's emphasis was intentionally placed on the power of form, mass and materiality.

Cape Town

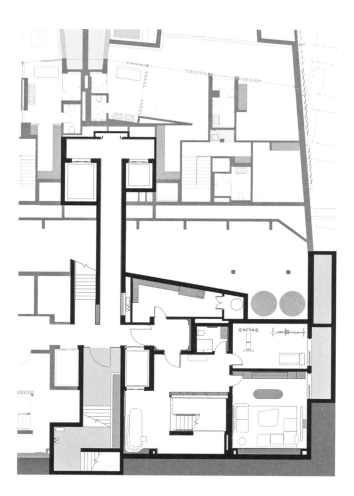

a

The dining area overlooking a large patio, raised pool and Clifton Beach.

b

The open plan living area displays furniture by OKHA, sculptures by Ben Orkin and Chantel Woodman and art by Mongezi Ncaphayi.

c

View into the bedroom.

d

The entrance lobby with a Shou Sugi Ban feature screen showcases bespoke artworks by artists Atang Tshikare and Chris Soal.

e

Ground floor plan.

f

In the guest bathroom, the visitor finds a bespoke hand-sculpted natural stone basin and marble clad walls.

284
285

# Cove

Interior design
Gaurav and Richard / Studio IAAD

Architecture
Rachna Agarwal / Studio IAAD

Location
North Goa, India

Year
2020

Gross floor area
464 m²

Number of bedrooms
3

This vacation abode for three friends in North Goa is conceptualized with three distinct clients at its nucleus, ensuring that each end-user felt tethered to the overall design narrative. An equilibrium of all their sensibilities, the residence shuns superfluous ornamentation for a rooted identity that reiterates the pleasures associated with unwinding in one's own private sanctuary. The site's level was lifted and leveled with the arterial road to offer seamless views of the waterfront. Responding to Goa's balmy, yet humid weather, the built volume has been imagined as a rooted and earthy structure amidst the dense plantations. Buff monochromatic travertine, sprinkles of white in various shades, patterned blue-pottery tiles and the umber wooden tones set the stage for the true coastal living experience.

North Goa

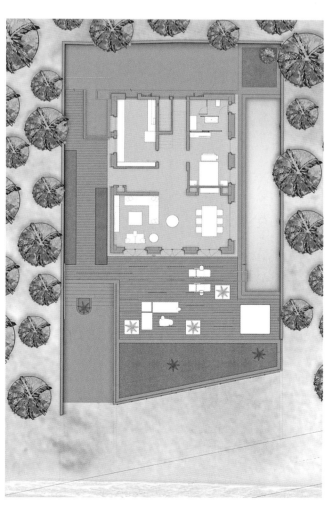

a
Living room with view of the sea.

b
Bathroom with natural materials.

c
Double-high dining area with view of the pool.

d
Exterior in lush nature.

e
Detail of bedroom.

f
Ground floor plan.

# CR Apartment

Interior design
ESQVTA

Location
Rua de S. Mamede, Lisbon

Year
2020

Gross floor area
315 m²

Number of bedrooms
3

The building in which this apartment is located, was originally planned as a Hotel Particulier. The apartment occupies the entire first floor. The task of the architects was to transform the floor, which has a historical character, into an apartment suitable for a family. The new program preserves the architectural heritage of the building and combines it with the needs of the family. In order to maintain and highlight the historical features, a careful selection of 21st century furniture was made. Thus, the interior design combines the 18th century features with high quality modern furnishings. The architects rewrite history with a new language and new pieces, keeping the main principle – a house to live in.

Lisbon

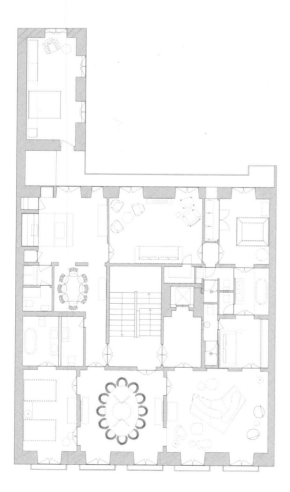

a
French windows open up to the street in the living room.

b
A majestic chandelier shines above the round glass table.

c
The living room shines in pastel colors combined with golden accents.

d
Light appearing curtains flank the TV-wall.

e
Floor plan.

f
In the bathroom the historical interior design appears to its best advantage.

# Index

# Index

# Index

# Picture Credits

Picture credits Cover: not applicable for special editions

# Imprint

The Deutsche Nationalbibliothek lists this publication in the Deutsche Nationalbibliografie; detailed bibliographic data are available on the Internet at http:/dnb.dnb.de.

ISBN 978-3-03768-274-6
© 2022 by Braun Publishing AG
www.braun–publishing.ch

The work is copyright protected. Any use outside of the close boundaries of the copyright law, which has not been granted permission by the publisher, is unauthorized and liable for prosecution. This especially applies to duplications, translations, microfilming, and any saving or processing in electronic systems.

1st edition 2022

All of the information in this volume has been compiled to the best of the editor's knowledge. It is based on the information provided to the publisher by the architects' and designers' offices and excludes any liability. The publisher assumes no responsibility for its accuracy or completeness as well as copyright discrepancies and refers to the specified sources (architects' and designers' offices). All rights to the photographs are property of the photographer (please refer to the picture credits).

Editor
Editorial Office van Uffelen

Editorial staff and layout
Lena Dagenbach, Maja von Hasseln, Nadja Spina

Graphic concept
Studio LZ, Stuttgart

Reproduction
Bild1Druck GmbH, Berlin